THE
POWER
TO
EXCEL

The book loaded with kinetic and positive energy
To empower. To inspire . To energize. To motivate

AZUKA ZUKE OBI

Dear Antonio Gagnon,

Live your dream, live big, live like a big personality. That's who you are. You are created to achieve big things. I am praying for you.

Azuka Zuke

4/1/14

DEDICATION

To my late mother, Joy, my friend, my teacher, motivator, and adviser whom I miss so much for her love, care, and for constantly reminding me of the power of determination. You were very cute, cared tirelessly for people, and were educated but still humble. You were spiritually dignified. You raised me with the strong belief in the power and goodness of the Lord. Before you went home to be with the Lord, Mum, you also told me to develop an attitude of gratitude and to give back and give at the slightest opportunity. Mama, I hold a place of gratitude in my heart in your honor, and I still love you even in death.

The Lord keep you safe in his hands.

HONORING JAMES SMITH

This page is created to honor Mr. James "Zimp" Smith, my humble senior, a proud Tuskegee Airman whose life has been a powerful source of inspiration to the younger generation.

Born in the state of Georgia, United States, on March 22, 1925, to Willis and Isabella Smith, James had eleven siblings comprised of six boys and five girls. He is the youngest and the only surviving member of this large family. His father, Willis, had died when James was only two years old. They were all involved in the share croppers business, dating back to his youth. According to James they were never paid until the end of the year, at which time they received their salary.

In the midst of the Great Depression, in 1933, together with his siblings, James moved to Jersey City, New Jersey, United States. He would always ask his mother why she moved them to New Jersey, where there was no food and it was very cold. That first winter was the first time in his life James had seen snow. There were no jobs, food was very scarce, and everyone was on welfare.

Times were very hard until the Second World War erupted on December 7, 1941. Japan had attacked Pearl Harbor, Hawaii, United States. There were not enough people to fill the vacant jobs in the country. The country needed manpower to fill the existing jobs and had to hire the black folks.

James enrolled in the US Army in 1943. In the US Army, James was one the few black folks that were enrolled in the famous Tuskegee program. He had received training at the Tuskegee College in Alabama, United States. When he came back from the army three years later, he realized that Jersey City was an all-white town and that more black people from the southern part of the United States, including Georgia, Alabama, and Mississippi, had been offered jobs in the defense factories. He saw that there was no diversity in the tavern business. So he hooked up with a friend named Manny, and they started doing business together. He took a loan from Manny and over time paid him off and continued his solo business for another thirty-five years. At one point James had twenty-two employees while creating jobs in America. He had three taverns and two restaurants all for thirty-five years. There were no computers, no Internet, no Facebook, no fax machines, nor Twitter. Everything about business records was manually kept on the ledger books. During this time period, James got married to his beautiful wife, Constance, and the union produced two beautiful children, Garrett and Dolores.

Garrett later became the first black mayor in Roselle, New Jersey. Dolores became an executive at Johnson & Johnson Pharmaceuticals and is in charge of the human resources in London, United Kingdom, and is happily married with children. James continued working hard up to his retirement and has been honored in so many different ways for his dedication and hard work.

On October 24, 2012, James was honored by the Office of the Clerk, Jersey City, New Jersey, in a resolution dedicating the southeast corner of Dwight Street and Ocean Avenue to be also known as James " Zimp" Smith Way.

—In-person interview with James "Zimp" Smith granted to the author

10/27/2012

ACKNOWLEDGEMENTS

I wish to thank all who have been part of my life and have blessed me with their presence. I acknowledge and show my respect to them for their support. For their concerns and generosity, I owe them my appreciation and sincere gratitude.

To my family for their support, love and inspiration.

For his generosity I thank Maxwell Chuks for being there during my university days in West Africa. Although he had his own financial challenges, he was always willing to spare me some change. I thank God for putting you in my path.

To all my teachers and professors whose trainings ignited the positive force within me, especially Dr. ST Ekeokoro. I have always been honored with your humility.

To Jean-Robert Baptiste, my brother and graphic designer,for his originality and patience in designing this book cover. Your skills are awesome. Your professional touch is just inspirational. Thank you buddy.

To Emmanuel Eze, Senior Pastor, The Guiding Light-Bromley Worship & Family Center (TGL-BWFC) , London, United Kingdom for his faith and moral support while I wrote this book. You constantly spoke to God on my behalf.

To Yvonne Ashby, who will always say things from her heart to encourage me. Yvonne told me never to quit and to write and continue writing till I publish. Yvonne believed so much in what I wanted to accomplish. Thank you Yvonne.

To Esther Chy Udeh for her positive energy. You called me every week to tell me to work extra hard and to rest only after I publish this book. You are a powerful source of motivation. Your energy is just unique.

To Terry-Ann Billups, Sildamise Pierre and Gladys Onatu for their friendship. You believe in me, encourage me, and motivate me to excel.

To Rev.James Moore.Sr, my pastor at Second Baptist Church, Roselle, New Jersey, USA. Your spiritual connection is just fantastic and is highly appreciated.

To Ofili Emmanuel, uncle, mentor, and confidant for standing by me all the way during the incubation, creation,and development of this book. You checked in often and congratulated me on every chapter I wrote. Thank you so much.

To Maha Farhat for being a practical example of motivation. Maha played a massive role in my drive to become an author. For your inspiration, your courage and above all, your generosity Maha, I thank you so much.

For his guidance and expertise, I salute Gaines Hill, my senior publishing consultant at Create Space, an Amazon company. You guided me through every question I asked in the process of publishing this book. Gaines is a living example of patience.

To Tara, my editor for doing a good job in reviewing my manuscript. You gave honest review and applauded me where I excelled. You motivate me when you wrote in your editor summary "Job well done". Thank you Tara.

Finally a very big thank you to my project team at CreateSpace for putting in time and skills to transform my manuscript into a powerful master piece at Amazon.com. Your speed in answering my questions and in guiding me through all the stages of the book publishing is unequalled. You all are awesome.

CONTENTS

FOREWORD

Growing up in a very small village in West Africa, I thought the world was going to collapse on me. However, having come from a very strong background and being a product of a highly disciplined culture, I have always believed that I was going to sail over the hurdles of life with determination. I did not by myself choose such a culture of rectitude for my childhood. It was imparted to me by my late mother, whom I miss so much, my father, my teachers, the community who at every point in my life provided me with strength, love, energy, and covering fire. I strongly believe that every leader is a product of their family, society, and community.

I found myself under the guidance and rules of very strict disciplinarian parents. I walked to school, often barefoot, at times in the company of my schoolmates. I received classes from unhappy yet underpaid teachers who could whip you silly at the slightest mistake of getting the wrong answer to the question. Having freedom of speech but the wrong answer was very costly. The code of conduct was just discipline. That was the society where I grew up.

I accompanied Mum to the market on Saturdays, trailing behind her like a baby goose, with a basket full of oranges, bananas and other fruits to be sold for my school fees. She was always there for me. Graduating high school was a rough road. Graduating from the university, a very Herculean task, was made possible by grants and scholarships as well as personal donations from kind-hearted individuals.

Coming to America was a big dream that masked obstacles and opened doors for advancement and personal growth. It also created a forum toward exploiting greater opportunities while expanding my capacity for pursuing the American dream.

Flying over Holland in Europe was a fascinating experience. I was airborne for the first time in my life. Sitting near a young white lady was an exciting experience. I recall not knowing what food to ask for from the air hostesses. My ears were very attentive to grasp the fast-paced accent of the Dutch flight attendant in between dozing off a couple of times to battle jet lag. It was a different time zone. I was flying to America.

Flying into the American airspace was not only fascinating but exciting. As I looked through the tiny window of the aircraft, I saw the Statue of Liberty standing tall in New York. I had a view of one of the world's most iconic skylines, a sweet memory of what I had seen only on TV and in pictures back home in West Africa. I had a smile on my face and little drops of tears down my cheek as I almost *landed in America.* There is nothing like landing in a city you are visiting for the first time. A few minutes later, the pilot announced our landing at the Liberty airport. It was a sweet sensation. Liberty to operate with freedom, liberty to express oneself, liberty to excel. And like every other person, I started my race in America, and over time the blessing descended upon me to write this book.

Oftentimes I ask, Why do people ignore the burning desire in them? Why do people fall short of their power to change things around to get to their destination? Opinions are divided as to what might cause this. Could it be that they are not willing to learn or that no one has ever fired up the zeal in them as to utilizing the power to maximize their potential? I have come to realize that the greatest people on Earth, be they astronauts, writers, engineers, actors, doctors, lawyers, agriculturists, foremen, pilots, and teachers, to mention but a few, have something in common. Each one has the "ignited power" in them.

By definition power is the zeal to drive, obtain, acquire, or possess anything. The power of "power" in guiding one's life cannot be underestimated. The moment you realize that you can have absolute power to control things in anything you do, the universe will, by a manner of induction, start to magnetize positive things toward helping you detect your inner energy to empower and guide you to the right track to excel in life.

Without the knowledge of the power in you, it becomes very difficult to acquire all the beautiful things that lie in stock for you. You have to, as a matter of urgency, ask the universe to guide you toward realizing your area of perfection. Once this is done, the road becomes very wide, and the width of each road you tread is a measure of the success that will follow thereafter.

It was not until I was in the second year of my university days that I realized that the power in humans can change lives.

This inspiration has burned in me for several years until I have come to terms with realizing the importance of putting this knowledge to good use, hence the birth of my book The Power To Excel

A lot of the greatest successes we have achieved are paralleled to the power in us. Teachers have created renowned engineers, lawyers, pilots and physical therapists because of the power in them. Architects have built mansions and other buildings spanning several stories based on the power in them. Scientists have developed various cures for various illnesses as a result of the vibe in their power. Prophets, on the other hand, can forecast the future based on the power in their DNA. The list goes on and on and without limit. The power to attract anything is a dynamic force in the universe that only a very few people are aware of and exposed to its application. You can be anything you want if you believe in the power in you.

I have come to realize that the more I think of anything on Earth—feel it, sing it, believe it —over time the magnetic power in me drives that into my mind, and I see it manifesting in the physical. If you want a new car, think a new car. If you want a new home, think a new home. If you want to be a successful business person, think like one, act like one. There would not have been any human history and discoveries if there hadn't been individuals who were willing to explore beyond their safe borders and do something out of their comfort zone. I empower you today to take that first step and change that stagnant routine, write that book, take that class, focus on that project, initiate that big plan, make that first public speech, embark on that journey, sing that song, enroll in that college. Give it all your energy, sell it to people, and watch what happens along the way. Do not be stopped by any resistance. The resistance you feel today was meant to keep you safe from tigers, but I can assure you right now that there are no tigers on your way to your destination. You are the only one that can stop yourself. As you read this little book written to empower you to be your best, may the power in you assist you to excel in life.

THE POWER EXPLAINED

THE WORD POWER HAS DIFFERENT MEANINGS depending on the context in which it is used. Power means the drive or ability to do something in a particular way as a faculty or quality. Power is defined as the capacity or ability to direct or influence others or the course of events. Another definition says power is a person or organization that is strong or influential within a particular context.

Scientists define power as the ratio of force to the surface area. According to physicist Isaac Newton, force combined with velocity equates to speed, which equates to power. This is the premise I will dwell on in this book. It means that a powerful person is one who has great speed and is in full control of their body. Power literally means the amount of strength you push into something with reference to the number of pushes that you apply irrespective of those that failed.

Without noticing or perceiving it, many people possess certain powers that move mountains throughout their lifetime. They go along life, wallowing in abject futility, swimming in total confusion, and searching for their destiny without ever realizing that the power to create their desired lifestyle lies within their being. Some people are fully aware of this power and utilize it to the best of their knowledge. Oftentimes the events of life drive us to recognize the innate power in us. To be able to use this power, you must first understand what power means, how it works, and what it can do. Start by saying "power, power, and power" up to ten times. Does it not feel powerful as you say the word power? Then start feeling that you have power in you. Feel the moving power in your system. Feel it, Feel it.

Feel it when you eat, when you run, when you smile, when you send an e-mail, while in the shower, in the kitchen, on the job, during church service, and in your subconscious mind as you sleep. Finally believing that you have power will induce power in you and set you off to taking powerful actions. You must have an intention, focus and goal for this to work. You must have a purpose for and a meaning attached to what you want to do. You must ask the "why" question. Ask yourself what you will do to make your heart loaded with joyful songs, to kick in that motivation, and to establish that "I can do it" attitude. These things give you, along with determination to excel, the confidence that you are on the right track and can take on any human being, challenges or anything that comes your way.

David from Bethlehem in Judah was confronted in a battlefield by the giant Goliath, a warrior from the city of Gath. David was able to disorganize Goliath because he totally believed in his power and, above all, the supreme power of his creator who manufactured him in his own image. Goliath was nine feet tall and wore a bronze armor that weighed about 125 pounds, a very heavy device.

Despite Goliath's intimidating showmanship, David was neither fearful nor moved. "You are coming against me with sword, spear, and javelin, but I come against you in the holy name of the Lord Almighty, the God of the Israelite armies, which you have defied. This very day the lord will put you in my power; and I will defeat you" (1 Samuel 17: 45). Note the words "my power." Do not forget that Goliath had challenged and oppressed the Israelites every morning and night for forty days, but it took David just a few hours to flush him out from the surface of the earth. To seal Goliath's chapter, David disrespected and renamed him "The heathen Philistine"—what an example of the power of confidence.

Human beings are created with innate powers from birth. Certain powers are so powerful that those who have them can change things within a split second. They are innately propelled at all times. Life is a very tough race that requires absolute energy, power, and faith to navigate. Events of life can often be devastating, but with a positive attitude, one can propel through it unscathed or if hurt but a little. History has taught us that humans have done great things because of the power and imagination emanating from their thought processes.

In the mastery world of human endeavor, whether in psychology, chemistry, astronomy, art, engineering, sociology, technology, earth science, or mathematics, people have discovered, created, and manufactured things that surpassed human imaginations, and as a result their names have been engraved indelibly in history. They believed and worked hard to achieve success. Sometimes the best thing to do is to just mimic an alchemist. Like an alchemist, you can transform something worthless into something valuable. The key to alchemy is in your perception, your visualization, your believe and your understanding of things. Sometimes it is about looking for the limitless possibilities and opportunities that surround you on a daily basis, seeing the innate and golden value of everything, and then turning that bitumen into gold. The best thing is to focus on what you want and on the people you want present in your life. Focus on the pure gold within each person you meet. You may have to overlook the visible bitumen to seek the hidden gold in them.

I personally have oftentimes found out that the more I use the power in me, the more it is developed and the more I feel fulfilled and accomplished. Wherever you are today, be it in Ottawa, Mogadishu, Denver, Freetown, Okinawa, Banjul, Rio, Kingston, Lagos, or Dakar, there is absolute power in you that can change things around you. These innate powers are all working in consonance with the universe. They move together, they are interwoven, and they are powerful. They are always in action. They have changed lives, they can change yours, and they can even attract things to you as long as you have the right frame of mind that is in alliance with the forces of the universe.

While still attending the university in West Africa, oftentimes it was very difficult to survive on the meager pocket money my late mother had always given me whenever I visited her from school. Following retirement from civil service as a teacher, she had relocated from the city with my father and provided me motherly care and love from the village. She also gave me pocket money whenever I visit from school. My brother supplemented whenever he could. I was preparing for my final examinations and had exhausted all my money on writing term papers, on books, on materials for my clinical presentations, and on transportation to and from the teaching hospital. My food allowance was at the lowest ebb. My morale was very low. To complicate matters, my roommate was hungry too. One night when I tried to prepare some food after having been very hungry all day at school, I realized that he had cooked and eaten the last noodles I had kept in my corner of the room. We shared dorm rooms in the university, and communal living was the order of the day. Everyone on campus lived like a family, so I had verbal paralysis and did not even dare question or get very upset at my roommate. I was very sad and felt knocked down. I felt so bitter that I had no money to carry me through to my final days at school. But then I decided to turn the situation around by feeling happy, singing a song (which became a "songito," our slang for song), playing my music, and dancing while being very grateful that I made it to the final days at the university.

I imagined myself having money again and even lent some out to fellow students. I continued in this frequency of gratitude and imagined myself becoming a little financially uplifted. I have always been blessed with some good smiles, and as the situation worsened, I smiled some more while every minute tapping into the charity of fellow students I had supported when my "morale" was very high. On campus everyone referred to money as "morale." I continued to radiate hope, success, and positive energy believing that I will be okay.

Two days after my roommate ate my noodles a distant uncle who had always supported me surprised and shocked me with an unannounced visit on campus. There was no way my uncle could've alerted me of his august visit. Information resources were limited. No student could afford cell phones, and none of us had one, not even our professors. A cell phone was a luxury only meant for and affordable by the "big boys." Sighting Uncle O was one of my happiest moments on campus, a memory that will live in me even when I die. Not only did he bring me some food, cases of bottled water, nice clothes, and matching classy hats, but he also loaded and rearranged my wallet with some change. Uncle was a successful business champion and always had some change to spare. My morale was very high once again. I did one quick dance, gave a victory sign into the air, alerted my good friends, and we ran celebrating. Later at night we popped some wine, drank, and thanked the universe for its wonders. I had money on me again and lived a little large in my last days at the university. I presented and successfully defended my papers, graduated, and moved on. Over time my believe in myself and the powerful attractive force in me got me a visa to live in and work in the United States where I am currently pursuing the American Dream.

No matter how rough the day may be, no matter how hopeless your situation mimicked mine while at the university, just imagine the best feeling with a positive and hopeful attitude. Not only will you change the situation, but you will do a quick dance like I did.

The way I used this power to attract my uncle and my migration to the United States is the same way ideas are attracted to our lives. When an idea flashes into your mind, there is always a power embedded with the idea. Your duty is to embrace the power and develop the idea. Our task as humans is not to control the myriad of ideas flowing into us. Rather it is to decipher what the idea is, how to work on it, and what the idea brings and then to strike it into a massive project.

Oftentimes we are too cautious and calculated about implementing our ideas. Or we are too busy analyzing how the idea will kick off and succeed. Every minute, ideas pop in our brains, but as humans we are degree holders in "analytical chemistry," and we analyze the ideas till the end of time. You die with the idea and are buried with eulogies referencing your dead idea. This same idea could have been given some life to enhance your time and presence on Earth. I see too much analysis as a hindrance and an impediment to the wheel of progress. When you expand an idea, you expand your capacity, you increase the flow of energy into your life, you sharpen your courage, and oftentimes you meet more people and learn more from them. The power in ideas is too big to be imagined. The car we drive today was someone's idea, as were the airplane, the ship, the telephone, the Mac Pro computer, the TV, the iPhone, the gas cooker, and the fax machine, to mention but a few. You don't have to figure out what the invention or the result of your idea will look like. Just use the power in the universe to strike the first shot, and every other thing will fall in place as you progress and the universe will support you.

I love the power in children. I learn a lot from them. When a child is given a bag full of colored cubes, squares, rectangles, and even rhombuses, the child goes straight to rearranging and building the different pieces. He does not look for guides, rules, or instructions to follow. He just starts working on the project irrespective of how it will turn out. Why can't adults use the same principle? Even when you fail in a project, never give up. Look for another idea that pops up and develop it. Oftentimes we get discouraged with a myriad of failures in making choices. Or we wait so long to start a project that we eventually forget the initial plan. I call this **"Personal Resistance."** It is a dream killer. It poisons your ideas.

It's personal in the sense that you are the one stopping yourself from taking action. Resistance can be very deadly. It is a dream killer. It is poisonous. It convinces you that you may not succeed or lists millions of imaginary requirements, funds, numbers, tools or connections needed in order to take off. Even when you start, resistance raises its ugly head again to stop you from moving on. But I empower you today to not give resistance a single chance. Set your speedometer in motion, and drive past the resistance. When you are in motion on the highway, no one can stop you. Even if the cops do, once you are cleared, you continue your journey. You can even take the next exit to avoid more delays from the state troopers, with a view to ultimately reaching your destination. That's how life works. You have to be in motion. This motion is the work needed to be done in order to see results. No matter how long you wait or prepare, please take action. Set yourself in motion. Take the first five yards with total determination, focus and believe, and the rest will fall in place as you move on. Then you can always figure other things out.

Every success story starts with somebody taking a small step. It could be sowing a small seed, which usually represents all you have at the moment. Simply stated, everything big starts with something small. In the Scriptures the servant who kept telling Elijah that nothing was happening finally saw something. It was just a tiny cloud, but it had great meaning and powerful potential. You can read on in 1 Kings 18:42-45. Remember that dynamite comes in small **packages.** This means that God loves to use things we think are insignificant to bring great surprises that changes life. But you must be willing to move and connect with the tools God uses. You must be ready to take actions and believe and work with faith.

"If you have faith as a grain of mustard seed, you shall say unto this mountain,move to another place; and it shall move; and nothing shall be impossible to you"- Matthew 17:20.

God used a boy's lunch to feed the multitude, a slingshot to bring down a giant, and a handful of clay to restore a blind man's eyesight.

He can use a little job, a little money, even information on a piece of paper or just a little idea to bless you. When God promises you something, he does not need anything big to make it happen. That's how he operates. I have seen it work in my life. The change that impacts the world starts with one person, be it Esther, or Paul, or Billy Graham, or Mathew or Mother Theresa. God uses one person who believes him and is ready to be used to impact the world. He uses those who believes in the tools he has available.

The key to success is simply to take action. Ideas grow when you spend time thinking of the ideas, visualizing the details, and planning and preparing their timely execution. Oftentimes people suffer from fear of failure, fear of what people will say or do, or from information overload. One popular Chinese proverb is "Talking will never cook the rice," meaning inaction will never achieve anything meaningful. Your action, resilience, perseverance, and authenticity are the leading forces that lead to success. You must be hopeful and always in the spirit of expectancy.

Never lose hope and be trapped in your poor choices. Accept changes with joy. The process of change is never rapid. It's a flow of incremental process. The key here is to be very patient and never give up. Big steps are made from small but calculated moves. Believe in your innate power, and hold your idea to a very high value with sincere intentions. Keep building up, gradually with dedication, faith, hope, and alliance with the creator. It won't be long before you strike the first gold. And when you do, I advise you to celebrate every victory, no matter how small, with gratitude. It is the right thing to do.

LITTLE CORNER

"Celebrate every victory, no matter how small, with gratitude"

THE POWER OF ACTION

POWER AND ACTION ARE VERY CLOSELY and positively related. Power possession leads to generation of action, which ultimately produces reactions and results. Individuals with power exhibit very great action potential, more than those who are power starved. This is not related to their social class or academic status but is a function of the vibe on the inside.

Power can be analyzed not only as a function of social structure but also as a force that can be set in motion by the right catalyst. Power possession leads to action, which ultimately attracts success. The powerful people are never constrained by societal obstacles but are propelled to success because they believe in their power and they take actions. They are not stopped by difficulties and are always in motion. They constantly turn up stones, searching for something underneath, and most times discover "gold." It is regrettable that many people have stumbled on the good stones but neither took action nor applied the principles to excel in their endeavors.

The power to have some money in your pocket, have that powerful relationship, put some food on your table, have a little change to spare to that homeless guy around the corner, to travel to live and work in America, to buy that dream house, or to finance that latest car you have been dreaming of is rooted deeply inside you. All it takes is to apply certain principles that are simple but very strict. Understand there may be difficulties and thorns on the way, but those are reversible. You can still achieve those things irrespective of the challenges that you meet on your path.

The power to either have a hopeless, disorganized, ruthless, catastrophic day or a powerful, fantastic, and productive day is in your hands. It is deeply rooted in your heart and is all about how you perceive and interpret the day. Everyone has the power to change the course their mind is heading on. I see life as a happy arena where each day must be enjoyed fully no matter what the circumstances are, even if it is the worst experience we could be in—death. Yes, death is very painful, especially when a dear friend or loved one passes on. But the key is to believe that God gives and takes away. It is okay to mourn for a time, but then move on and continue being productive. Enjoy life with a view to forging ahead on daily basis. It may sound difficult, but I can assure you that once you are ready to move on, God will move on your behalf to give you a renewed energy to fire on. The key is to feel good about that which you want for yourself. Send out the love to the universe, and continue to believe it with all your heart, and it won't be long before you will receive that which you believed. You can always attract anything you want. The powers are embedded in the laws of attraction. They are universal laws. They are very powerful. They can change your life from disgrace to amazing grace as long as you are willing to connect listen to your inner being, your thoughts and your mind.

The human mind is flooded with a myriad of ideas on a daily basis. These ideas could be little or could be big but all of them have powerful potentials. Oftentimes one of the things that causes delay when you have ideas is that inability to act and develop the idea. Oftentimes we are presented with fear, but once you think beyond the fear and act and follow up diligently with patience, you will ultimately see results, and your fears will disappear. You do not have to wait endlessly for that perfect idea to come to mind. There is no perfect idea. Rather you can get to work immediately, research more on the idea, and turn things around while creating opportunities for growth. Oftentimes people have good ideas but they stop searching when their ideas fail. They lose hope and give up. But the key is to continue searching and believing. I can assure you that if you continue trying, working hard and believing it won't be long and one will click and fall in place, but you never know which one. So the key is to spread out your dragnet as you progress. Initially you may be too myopic to see where you are going, but ultimately you will get to the right place. It will only take some time but you will get there.

Successful people make decisions and act no matter how many times they fail. They don't wait for years to act; they don't quit when the going gets tough and rough or when they fail a hundred times. They make instant decisions and take actions. They are like the hunter in an African forest infested with dangerous animals. They don't postpone their decisions to be very alert. They know full well that one dangerous move or one minute of a shift from focus could allow a wild animal to devour him and make dinner of his body. Most people pass through life without making any impact because they never direct their focus and concentrate on the power in their being. They focus on things that drain their energy. They engage in negative thoughts. They gossip, they are very busy interfering in matters that do not concern them. They parade news of events in town. They focus on rubbish and are distracted by the daily events of life. They settle for mediocrity and with whatever flow that life brings. They lack focus, they have low morale, their determination is paralyzed, and they end up achieving nothing. They blame lack of time for their deficiencies. People who are or want to be successful are always focused. They always channel their energy to the right stuff that will enhance their lives toward making a difference and succeeding. They want to succeed. They think positive, act positive and possess drive channeled towards positive movements. They are happy because they are very productive. They get positive results. Are you on the negative or the positive side?

I challenge you now to stop what you are doing right now. Drop this book you are reading now, shut off your cell phone, and turn off the television if it is on and silence every background noise. Then write down just two things that can reform and change your life if you focus on them starting now. Then write down ideas that you could inject into these two things to expand them and make them realizable. Then start working on these every day by doing those things that will give life to the ideas. When you do this you are taking small steps towards making positive changes and enlarging your horizon. You are re-branding your life and chances are that You could be very successful too.

Successful people are focused, and they make quick and sharp decisions. They decide, they ask for God's blessings, they act, they stick to their decisions, they fire on full cylinders, and they dare any circumstances on Earth to challenge them to fail. Even when they fail, they move to the next project and open a new chapter of ideas without fear. They learn from their experience, believing that experience and action beats failure every time. With a few positive adjustments and a refusal to quit, they excel. Successful people are always in motion. This is called kinesiology, meaning "the science of human motion."

I remember Paul once said to the Philippians, "There is one thing that I do: I forget the past, I press forward to what lies ahead." In essence Paul was saying, "I don't care what has happened. I am pushing and pressing on. I don't want to be negative and stuck in one place. I am firing on and moving forward and toward the prize, and I will excel. I am taking actions." I learnt a lot from Paul's principle of forging ahead and believing. If you believe, so shall it be. If you think you are a loser, you will be a loser. If you think you will be a winner, you will be a winner. Take action today, and change something. But first you have to change and if possible connect with people who will want you to succeed and people who will support you.

I advise you to take action and find and connect to people who will always tell you, "You will make it." People who will keep you focused on what is important. People who will be with you and support you even if your plan fails.People who will constantly remind you that you have a right to succeed. Stay away from hopeless and negative people. Do not give them a room in your brain's house; instead increase the rent five times, and they will move to a cheaper neighborhood where they will be totally away from you.

High-powered individuals exhibit a very high level of confidence. They is more inclined to succeed. They believe in their power as an invaluable asset and property. They take actions. If you want to win the Olympic marathon, you must start by practicing running to build cardiovascular endurance. Train in dry, wet, and humid weather. You may even hire a personal trainer to build your cardiovascular endurance and improve on your energy level. Then progress to your local community 5K run, then 10k. Then take the next action step by joining other successful runners in practicing running many miles in cold, warm, hot or humid weather Sounds rough, eh? But that's the key to success.

In essence, activating power activates action. Possessing power leads to action. This is a fact. How does power lead to action? Your power enables you to engage in actions that facilitate success, accomplishments, and progression in life. Having power leads to strong action. Having no power leads to inaction, which ultimately brings little or no results?

At birth we only have two fears: fear of falling and fear of loud noises. As a child these two things are our only fears. Yet as toddlers we run, jog, dive, jump, and even cross to the cabinets in our homes without fear of falling or something hitting us. We take bold actions irrespective of the consequences. We dream big. But as we grow up, we become fearful. We slack. We stop taking actions. We pick up many things to fear along the course of life. We fear "fear" itself.

One of the benefits of taking actions without the fear of failing or falling is that it won't be long before fear shows up. This is a positive sign. Knowing that it will show up is a good indication that your actions will succeed. Then you get ready to counter the fear. Oftentimes you will find yourself thinking, "I can't do this. I will embarrass myself. I will fail in this action. How will I get started? I don't know how much time it will take or who will help me. I don't think I can do it." But you can initiate the good emotions running in your blood telling you, "I can do this. I am equal to the task. I will pull this one off, I must accomplish this task."

Fear is your emotions that lie to you and tell you to stop, chicken out, and quit. But I urge you today to stare that invisible fear in the face and declare, "With faith I can do this. I will strike it big, It is in my DNA to succeed, get behind me, fear." Tell yourself, "I am smart. I am energetic. I am solid. I am powerful. I am curious. I am fearless. I am determined. I am creative. I am focused. I am solid. I am renewed. I am authentic. I am ignited. I am activated. I am fully packaged. I am motivated. I am prepared. I will succeed." Gather all the entire positive "I ams" you can think of and pronounce them into your life. Write and paste them in places where you will see them every day. Read them aloud while you brush your teeth, while you walk to the kitchen, and while you relax in your bedroom. These are natural statements that you create to match the fear in you. Pull your actions with determination, with no fear or favor, then watch and see them excel. Find the right positive statements that match your fears and projects, and compose them into a song and sing it daily until it masters your thinking. Sing it when you wake up, while talking a walk, when you are in the store, when you are at the gym, on the bus, at your lunchtime, inside your heart during church service, in the kitchen, in the living room, and even when you are sleeping.

There has been a great belief in the power of denials and affirmations since the beginning of life because it is the practical truth. If you deny, you fail. If you affirm and believe, 99 percent of the time you will succeed.

Fear is not a sign that you are doing something out of the ordinary or wrong; it is a sign that you are out of your comfort zone, taking bold actions, and igniting positive moves to reorganize, rebrand, and rewrite the story of your life. Do not stop. Keep taking actions. There is power in taking actions. When you act, reactions take place, and people react and most times they provide massive support.

Isaac Newton, a disciple of the great physicists, taught us that action and reaction are equal and opposite. This means the amount of action you apply is equal to the amount of reaction you generate. Something happens when you apply actions in extraordinary ways and with determination.

Is there something you are dreaming about but you don't seem able to take action to do it? Are you stuck using the same pattern every time? It is time to take action and take control of your life.

People already know how to build a house, gain college admission, or train for the Olympics, but most people never take the necessary action to achieve them. If you desire to be a college graduate, get your high school diploma first, then apply to that college. That's the first action. Action is practical work, not merely theory or paper work.

Why do people act in ways that negate their progress? Because they live in a "mental prison" devoid of actions. They admire successful people, wish to be like them when they are like them already, but refuse to take action to live like them. All it takes is to believe you are like them and fire the first shot—action. Many people don't take action because of the comfort in their familiar territory. Change requires action and bold steps to challenge a new discomfort, fear, or uncertainty. Initially it could be very scary and rough, but once you get used to it and are willing to adjust and accept the transient discomfort, it won't be long before you touch, feel, and enjoy the awaited benefits. You can never live your best life without action, change, sacrifice and discomfort. This is my belief!

Life has taught me that where there is action, there is opportunity. Every day we hear of success stories because someone decided to take action with a view to working very hard to reach their target goals. I encourage you to do something different today to enhance and make your life better. The idea that you have been nursing inside you for years could be the rolling stone that gathers momentum and could change your life for good.

If you are not taking actions, you are not growing and you are not creating opportunities. It is like you are trying to catch a lobster in your backyard without going to the Atlantic Ocean. You know this is impossible. Most people fail because they stop taking actions. They stop trusting their actions, and they lose hope and abandon their lives to fate. Do not be one of them.

Everyone on Earth has a unique gift. Your gift to the world will be the uniqueness of your God-given talent for creating , improving yourself and impacting others. You are a gift to the world. Make the best use of that gift.

Engage in something new, get seriously involved in a plan, make that long-term commitment to shine in a project, and start taking actions. Are there things you have been wanting to do or projects you have been wanting to execute. Is there a song you have been planning to sing? You don't have to wait for Usher to sign you on his label. You can start little, even by singing in your home church. I empower you to start something today. Accomplish those personal goals, meet those powerful people, start that movement,and I assure you that you are on your way to making an impressive mark on the universe and creating massive opportunities for growth.

Make a short list of goals and aspirations that you have for your life, write them down, and read them with humility and hope everyday in the morning before you kick off the day's activities. This will serve as a constant reminder that they are the things you desire to accomplish and will make it easier to work on them. Make them your "now" and "every day" recital. Check them off as you execute them. As you progress and succeed, please celebrate every little success. Make plans today believe it, intend it, sing it, pray it, and get out of that mental prison and comfort zone. Start something today.

There are golden opportunities everywhere, but you have to make the first move to grab them. Any place where people are gathered together with one positive energy, you will find someone waiting to present you with opportunities. Immigrating to America a few years ago opened powerful opportunities for my advancement. Today I have a charity fitness program where I am expanding my capacity, changing lives, developing fitness, and giving back to the community by using fitness as a positive force. Margaret Meade put it better: "Never doubt that a small group of thoughtful, committed citizens can change the world."

You have to find the right people to guide and assist you step by step in piloting your actions. Find friends who motivate you, and hang around them always. Connect with people who:

- will resonate, celebrate and empathize with you
- will hear you and answer you and are very useful and less elusive from you.
- blend well in your atmospheric climate and support you
- are dynamic, loyal and people who feel you
- welcome your creative differences while enhancing a positive and friendly atmosphere and willing to see you excel
- sense when you are deviating and losing focus from set plans
- connect with you emotionally and encourage you throughout your race in life.

Keep away from toxic people and relationships. Avoid those who have nothing to offer in your relationship and are negative." If you hang around them, you may be infected by their poison. The best thing to do is to disconnect from their useless and negative energy and take positive actions for your life and future. Take action today to re-new and re-charge your mental, physical, emotional, ethical, moral, and financial capacity. When you take actions the universe moves on your behalf, God steps in working behind the scenes in your favor and you see positive things coming to your life, you see changes and your life takes a new turn for good. Take action, it is very important. Remember it is the action part that disables most people. Do not be one of them.

LITTLE CORNER

"There are golden opportunities everywhere, but you have to make the first move to grab them."

THE POWER IN US

EXPERIENCE HAS TAUGHT ME THAT A person's innate power can oftentimes lead to a very fruitful life. Growing up, I oftentimes realized that a few things I desired would come my way whenever I focused on it, prayed about it, sang about it, and dreamed about it. This was a manifestation of the power in me. I had never been good at using my innate power, so even when I took control of my thoughts and actions, I still wasn't too hopeful.

But as I continued to practice on a daily basis the process of owning and managing my thoughts, I made several realizations. I realized that inside every human being lies the power to create things and that I am capable of creating more than I have imagined. I started to realize that with the right mindset, practice, and patience, there is a lot that everyone can imagine and create that they've never done.

Do you think you missed the band's world singing tour only because you did not master singing while in high school? Have you always thought it would be cool singing for the first time in front of a multitude of people? Or have you wanted to do a surprise dance at the retirement party of your company's director without minding what people think of you or the dance steps? If you try it for the first time for fun, I can assure you will be amazed how your possibilities can expand drastically. Remember you are not competing with or trying to impress anyone; it is about trying something ordinary in an extraordinary way for fun.

You may not perform perfectly and not everyone may like it or sing or dance along with you. But if you like your act, you better step it up, give it life, stand out, and do your thing. When you give yourself freedom to mess up at something that makes you feel rather good, excited, and happy while doing it, then you create mental freedom for yourself and enhance avenues to maximize your action potential, and live fully with a view to succeeding in your acts. And guess what? You are preparing your fireworks for bigger things. You are building confidence while becoming popular in your acts. Make it a daily routine to stretch your mind with something very new and something that makes you happy. No knowledge is a waste and you have no idea what your knowledge and acts can transform to. It is never too late to learn. You can always train yourself to and act the way you want and receive what you want.

The same concept applies to physical things. If I need a new shirt, then I envision a shirt, and I'll receive a new shirt as a present. It does not matter who gave it to me. The bottom line is that I received a new shirt. A new pair of shoes will land in my hand if I focus on it constantly for a few days. It does not matter if I bought the shoe or someone else did, the point is that I have a new shoe. Whenever I think seriously of a person, the next phone call comes ringing from that person or someone who knew the person and wants greetings extended to me. I have always thought of becoming an author and publishing my first book in America and today is a reality with the publication of this book.

I was thinking of buying a Honda CRV car in 2006. I focused on it for ten days, prayed at the same time each day, and by the eleventh day, I was cruising in my car, feeling accomplished. The same process got me my third car, the Jeep Liberty truck that I drove to the launch of this book.

When my Windows Vista-based computer was about to retire, I knew it was time to step up. I felt it especially when it shut down on me with reckless abandon. I felt the need to advance to a Mac computer. I knew God wanted me to be "Mac-ed" up. I took time in my private, peaceful location to focus on, think of, and "feel" my new computer. I imagined logging into it and browsing the Internet, after which I shut it off and put it safely in a corner of the house. Remember, this new Mac computer hadn't existed physically, but I was using it and feeling it. I did this for twenty days, and by the twenty-third day, the designer of this book's cover, told me that we had to go to the Apple Store to window-shop for computers. He had seen my worn out PC a few weeks earlier and was not impressed. By the time we left the Apple store, I had purchased a brand new Mac Pro computer. I browsed and e-mailed all night with joy and gratitude in my heart.

Whatever it is that you desire in life is very achievable if tackled with a positive mindset. Oftentimes we neglect the rich abundance of our innate power and, as such, miss so much of life's blessings.

Muhammad Ali, born Cassius Clay, believed in his own power and attracted fame, honor, medals, and glory, not to mention the huge amount of money he accrued in his boxing career. He is known in Uganda, Haiti, the US, Australia, Fiji, Brazil, and Greece. He is known everywhere. In the Summer of 2012 in London, he was honored as a goodwill ambassador of the Olympics. Soccer star Pelé of Brazil was in love with his own power and today lives as the greatest soccer legend of all time.

Joel Osteen strongly believes in his power and today ranks among the top three powerful evangelists on Earth. His ministry is still spreading and waxing strong day by day, and I am tuned to his frequency every week. He energizes, motivates, and empowers me.

The Ghana Black Stars, the national soccer team of Ghana, a West African country, united for once in the history of African soccer and almost made it to the semifinals of the 2010 senior World Cup held in South Africa.

History will never forget Barack Obama, an American citizen son of an immigrant African man, who became the first black president of the United States of America.

Michelle Obama became the number one black first lady of the United States because she believed it was possible and today still keeps a very humble but powerful profile while championing her cause to reduce childhood obesity. Quite understood she was a Harvard and Princeton University graduate but her believe was the major factor in her success despite her humble beginnings.

Dr. Maya Angelou, an influential voice and positive force survived the brutality of racism with her unshakable faith and today is a poet, novelist, educator and ranks among the great black historians of the American nation. Maya had several impact on humanity all over the world including Africa. Her work and legacy will continue to be a powerful source of inspiration to the younger generation. Maya is an example of the woman power.

Through these examples we see that it is crystal clear that the power in us as humans can change anything. All you need to do is believe. " And all things ,whatever you shall ask in prayer believing , you shall receive "-Matthew 21:22

The Scriptures teach that when two people are gathered and praise God in a genuine way, there is an answer. Paul and Silas sang and prayed together, and the Holy spirit came down. In essence everything that one turns in the direction of God is a prayer. If you teach a young one how to apply life's principles to succeed, you are praying. If you lend a helping hand to a neighbor who is in need, you are praying. If you are grateful for what you have now, you are praying. If you spare that homeless guy some change for his next meal, you are praying. Never miss any opportunity to make some small sacrifice. For your charity and almsgiving to others there is always a divine blessing. An apple given during life is more profitable than a stadium full of wreaths and diamonds given after death. God has no need for your money nor treasures. When you give it to the needy, God receives. For me prayer means being grateful for all the things I have now, including being able to talk, see, and hear (especially when others speak) and my ability to give at any time to those who need my help and services. The effects have been tremendous in my life. When you give, you open doors for more blessings. It is a natural law.

One important thing in the lives of extraordinary people is the belief they had in their power to excel. They could experience trials, rough roads, and tribulations, but all the success stems from their innate power and their desire to succeed. When you dissect the principle of resurrection critically, you will understand better the teachings that God will always finish whatever he started. No matter how rough your road is, no matter how dark the tunnel is, irrespective of the number of people trying to run you down or defame your character, if you will stay in faith and believe in the power of God, he will always pilot you in everything you set your mind on , guide you and will complete that which he started in you. He will bless you.

Steve Harvey believed in himself when he decided to become the best stand-up comedian in America. Steve, in 1985, with the power of belief, quit his two jobs as an insurance salesman to pursue what he believed in: becoming the best comedian. That single belief of wanting to be the best propelled him in measures that cannot be equaled. Of course there were tribulations on his path to success. At some point he was so broke that he lived in his car while moving from place to place to perform. One thing is clear: all his greatness stems from having that desire and believing in his innate power. He believed and topped it with faith, and great things started happening in his life. The same is applicable to you if you work hard and believe.

Let's take a trip down memory lane a little to see more classic examples of the power of belief and absolute faith. Over two thousand years ago or more, according to Scripture, *Peter believed with faith and got a big basket of fish. Joseph believed with faith and became a great and respected governor in a foreign land even after his brothers, who he trusted and loved so much, had betrayed him, put him in harm's way, and possibly planned his funeral. David believed and, fighting with faith, conquered the huge and fearless Goliath; today David's name is etched forever in the annals of the confident and powerful ones. I christened him the "tiny bulldozer." Sampson believed with faith and pulled down the mighty building. History will never forget Paul and Silas who, even in adversity, sang, rejoiced, prayed, and believed with faith and received one of the greatest gifts on Earth: freedom.*

I empower you to just believe in yourself and in everything you set your mind to accomplish with faith. That's all you have to do and God will take care of the rest. There is no special formula for faith. It is not like any complicated physics or mathematical equation. It is not calculus or algebra. It is a very simple two-word formula: …"have faith." It is simply unseen; it is the substance of things you imagine by yourself for yourself. To make it even more simple, understand that you are not expected to have faith as big as the New York City bus or as giant as the European Continent but just a little faith as small as a mustard seed. In essence you just have to believe in whatever you are doing.

We as individuals can always set and visualize the dreams we want to achieve. Life is like a vision, but oftentimes we are doomed when the vision becomes foggy. Many people are the best in what they do. We all handle challenges in different ways. Believing in one's power is a powerful tool for attaining success. The key is believing and never doubting your goals and aspirations. Oftentimes many people get intimidated and slow down whenever things don't go their way. They lose hope, they freeze, or things become cloudy, unclear, and unknown. I have learned that hoping with faith can lift that heavy load of disappointment and will create ways to raise you above the clouds of uncertainty that have limited and tainted your horizon.

I read of a woman whose several rejection slips almost shattered her dreams of becoming an author. But she had a dream and would not want to be defined by other people, so she decided she would do anything possible to get her book published. She self-published her novel electronically through Amazon.com. She sold a few copies the first day, a few more the second day, and continued selling. She continued writing and released subsequent books. Today she is a very successful author. She even got traditional book publishing deals. There is no special formula for success. There is no advanced university degree for success. Success is only a function of dedication, struggles, hard work, learning, falling, rising, persistency, and consistency.

Another powerful factor in creating success is the ability to make and accept change. Change can happen to anyone and at anytime. By the power of change and your willingness to change on the inside, you can create new things. Change can make all things new again. Change can alter lives and create way for advancement. But for this to happen, you must have life-changing principles. The first principle is that you must be very prepared and willing to change unconditionally. This change first must be from within and must be well intended. Then the universe controlled by God's power provides the ultimate reward and gift that awaits a changed person. Then you see things from a clear perspective, understand problems better, deal with them effectively irrespective of their magnitude, and then rise and excel.

This brings us to visualization, or, better still, "visual conditioning." Visualization means forming a mental image of something. Visualization is an intrinsic power in every individual. Even babies have it. Visualizing your future will help you achieve your life's goals. What do you see in your future? Where are you going, and what are your goals? What little thing will you do today to move nearer to your aspirations? I can assure you that little things done consistently over time will be the channels that enhance your road to excellence. Oftentimes the simplest decisions lead to miracles. You should constantly set small goals, then big goals, while constantly evolving with a view to opening up greater opportunities.

But for opportunities to flow there must be people—not just people or hopelessly negative people, but positively minded people. Not everyone who comes with you can work effectively with you. Some people are there for a reason, some for one day, some for one season, and some for two seasons. Some are there for a few years and some for a life time. Those with very short but useless and selfish intentions should be cut off from your friendship. Some people should be let go after awhile, or they will poison your positive energy. There is always a way to remove toxic friends from your system. If a friendship is not energetic and encouraging, it is not worth keeping. Conversely, if you have to give yourself a mental pep talk and spiritual preparation before you meet or visit, that's a sign to watch out for a poisonous and useless friendship. If you hang around negative people, I advise you to either be ready for a downward turn of your life and negativity or just disengage yourself from that relationship. For me I have zero tolerance for useless and negative people. If you mingle with lions, you will learn how to be a carnivore, but if you associate with eagles, you have no option but to fly. Anyone who doesn't appreciate you or your efforts, encourage you, or is not reliable is not worth having around. I refer to them as associates or acquaintances. They are definitely not your friends and can disorganize and slow you down. They can deflate your tires on the interstate highway of life.

To be successful among friends, you have to find out the reason for the friendship. People become friends for different reasons: association, respect, admiration, convenience, or benefits. Above all it is easier to develop and maintain strong friendships with people you respect and/or who respect you and share strong and beneficial values with you. These people are positive in all aspects of their lives.

Associating with positive people will not only encourage you but will also set your mind right. You must have the right mindset before great things can start flowing into your life. You have to display a positive attitude. Having a positive attitude is very crucial in your relationships, on the job, in the way you relate with others, in your family, and in the charity movement you are championing. Positivity is also crucial in the way you interact with people, including your neighbors, and in the way you pilot your life on the path to excellence and success. If you are still struggling with maintaining a positive attitude, the best thing to do is to align yourself with at least one positive and upbeat person. The mentor who introduced and opened my eyes to the power of positive attitude always told me to act like I am in a hurry. That was twenty years ago. He was right then and is still right and I believed him. As I practiced acting hurried, I started to realize that people love to associate with people who are moving on and have an attitude of urgency. Why is this? Because active and urgent persons always get results. They are always creating positive moments. Their lives are full of excellence. They make things happen, and they motivate, energize, and empower others to succeed along their way.

When I did this for five years I saw that different types of people were following me as I moved including those much older than me. I realized that I am very important and meant a lot to people and that I could influence and impact their lives. My life took a new dimension. If you do the same for some time or even longer than me, you will find out that as you look backward you will surely find people following you, like on Twitter. Guess what? You are powerful. You have a positive attitude. You are successful. You have become a leader. But most people make the mistake of wanting to become leaders in the wrong way. They think that they have to have that big title before they can learn how to be a leader. They do not know that showing leadership skills without any strings attached is the way to earn that big title. They do not understand that leadership is not a position but a long-term process of service. When you are serving, you are a leader.

I make lots of jokes, and I do not want anyone in my life who brings with them only selfishness and takes advantage of the joy of my company. That will never happen. Through my life so far, I have been very fortunate that God has surrounded me with positive people who care deeply about me, my aspirations, and my dreams. Even before this book was published, they have always motivated and empowered me to be the best I can be. They encouraged me to write, write, and continue writing till I published. They keep an eye on me.

Decide today what small things you can do to enhance your life and that of others. After all, dynamite comes in small packages, and small actions in the face of great troubles can change things. But you must be ready to make good and strong decisions. Making decisions involves believing in yourself, figuring out how to do something, taking actions, knowing the price that will be paid, and then going deep to pay that price. Having a successful life involves positive actions and not wishful thinking. Ninety-seven percent of the time, we devise a plan, we study the plan, plan the study, appreciate the plan, plan the appreciation, get excited with the plan, and analyze the plan, but we never execute the plan. Others will start, but when the first month doesn't go well, they freeze and stop, and the idea dies. A person venturing into a new business will want success very fast, but things don't happen that way. When there are no customers or the product doesn't sell well, he quits and gives up hope. The business shuts down. One thing is very clear: you can only fail if you quit. If you don't quit, chances are that you will excel. Remember you have "The Power to Excel."

If you want to start that new dream job, open a supermarket business, run at the Olympics, write a book, venture into modeling, make that first motivational speech, or sing your first solo at church, then be ready for the setbacks. The first time I sang a solo in my local church was very challenging. I had never done it in America. A little nervous, I saw some people laughing because I never sang in church before, neither am I a choir member. I suspected some people thought, "he will blow it." But guess what? I was neither intimidated nor distracted—I sang. I sang because it never mattered to me to look at their faces. The song was not for them, or about me, or my pastor, but for my creator who gave me a voice to sing. I will continue to sing. If I had thought about what people would say or their reactions, I may not have achieved my personal goal of singing during a live Sunday service in my home church. The key here is to do your thing irrespective of people's reactions or setbacks.

The setbacks are part of the process of succeeding. The false starts, the miscalculations, the fear, the failures, and the challenges are all part of the success stories that you tell later. The challenges could be financial. It could be physical. You may even have to travel thousands of miles with neither enough funds nor the assurance of a roof over your head upon arrival. They are all the price of success. Coming to America gave me the opportunity of becoming an author.

It is wishful thinking that you can plan and execute a project so well without setbacks. In fact the bigger the project, the more obstacles you encounter. The important part of the process is that you have to ignite the power in you to initiate and make that change. It can be tough, uncomfortable, and ruthless, but guess what? It is all part of the price.

Surmounting the problems on the path is the process that changes you to ensure the success of the project and to make you become a better person. Whether big jobs or small jobs, big projects or small projects, successes are all achievable. The power lies in you. You can only fail if you quit.

LITTLE CORNER

"If you lend a helping hand to a neighbor who is in need, you are praying."

THE POWER OF CONFIDENCE

"REMEMBER THAT I HAVE COMMANDED YOU to be determined and confident! Do not be afraid or discouraged, for I, the Lord your God, am with you wherever you go"-Joshua 1:9.

Confidence is the ability to believe in oneself at all times. It is a reflection of who you are, a manifestation of your image. It is believing that you can do and achieve anything. Confidence defines you as an individual and is related closely to your chances of succeeding. What is the level of your confidence? Are you of zero confidence? Are you averagely confident? Are you super confident or laser confident? The option is yours. No one is born confident, but no matter where you find yourself, you can always build on your confidence; you can be better. You can always improve on your confidence. You can command whatever level of confidence you desire. You can learn it, you can practice it, and you can live it.

If you do not know how to do it, you can model and copy others who have it.

You can watch motivational speakers, pay attention to your pastor when he preaches and your professors. Their confidence got them in front of people. Learn how they do it , how they talk and move their hands and then add your own idea and do your own rehearsals in front of the mirror and then your trusted friends who can honestly criticize you and make corrections.

One simple way to learn is to assume simple leadership roles in your immediate family, your church, school or even on the job. By taking responsibilities and addressing a small a group of people and delegating duties you can build confidence. Physical appearance affects confidence as well. If you dress sharp you feel good outside and inside as well. If you dress shabbily chances are that you feel bad and this may impact your interaction with people. But you don't have to spend all your money on expensive clothes. The point here is to dress sharp and look sharp and by so doing you feel good on the inside and this is translated in how you operate.

The way you walk tells a lot about you. To build confidence, walk like you are in a hurry to see someone or catch up on something. Walk with your shoulder high. Walk like an important personality which you are. You will find out that people are admiring and copying you. Nobody wants to copy someone who walks with no energy. This will help build your confidence. Physical fitness has a lot to do with your level of confidence. Working out helps build strength and energy levels and puts you in good shape. Your good shape and fitness boosts your confidence.

The pictures that flash into your mind daily are so powerful and interconnected with your level of confidence. You are the most solid and confident person on Earth, and your personality is a reflection of the confidence you charge into the atmosphere.

The level of your confidence is proportional to the level of the success you portray. Confidence gives you the extra boost to take on challenges and take risks. Your confidence is portrayed when you stand in front of a crowd to talk, when you sing to the public, when you call for a meeting with your supervisor, when you take on the leadership role in your family, and when you believe in yourself and in everything you do.

Most people are held back from developing the myriad of ideas flowing into their brain because they lack confidence. They do not have faith in themselves. They don't believe in themselves, and they do not want to learn from others. Even when they find an answer to a question they have asked all their lives, they discard it because they do not believe the answer will work in their favor or conclude the answer is not meant for them.

But I have always advised people to ask themselves this confident question: "If other people can do this, why can't I do it too?" The answer is you can do it if you believe it and put your time, energy, and focus in it and do it with confidence and humility. You can even do better than they did. The only thing that stops you is your lack of total belief in yourself. Sometimes it is because you are thinking too much about what people will say or do when you make that first positive move. But I can assure you that once you make that first move, the universe will pull good people, resources, gifts, and support to offer all you need to enable you to shine and succeed.

The vibrations of your confidence stimulate sensory signals that attract people and success proportional to the amount of energy and confidence you put in. Confidence is a gradual and steady process. It does not happen in a day. It is a journey that is achieved one little step at a time. When you have confidence, you know where you are going, you have a goal, and you have a plan. You determine to succeed.

Confident people respect people a lot but fear nobody. They have absolute faith in God and in themselves. They are creative. They are always in motion. They walk as if they are in a hurry. They tackle challenges head on. They know that in as much as there are obstacles on their way and that there are stumbling blocks around them that they cannot control, they can control how they react to those challenges. They work hard with confidence and have no option but to excel. They turn stumbling blocks into stepping stones and transform disgrace into amazing grace. They are alive. They have vision and are never myopic. They see opportunities that lie in front of them. They make things happen. They have faith in their lives. They put their trust in God.

Every human being, including me (point your second finger to your heart now), has solid potential. They only need to believe in themselves. With this in mind, I empower you to raise the bar today and decide on one thing you want to start, with faith that you will succeed in it. Discard all the useless reasons you give for not starting, and make that first move with confidence.

Soccer teams with good training coupled with confidence and who play according to game plans have a very big chance of winning a game. The confidence exhibited by the Ghana Black Stars in the 2010 FIFA Soccer World Cup in South Africa earned them a berth into the quarterfinals, making them the second African country to reach the quarterfinals of the senior soccer World Cup. Remember they may not have come to the tournament with the world's best players, but they came with confidence boldly written in their hearts.

Born in Kentucky, United States, in 1942, the great Muhammad Ali was able to win most of his boxing fights during his career. Although he trained, worked out, and fought hard, his confidence in the ring was key to making him the greatest fighter that ever lived. Known for his pre-match gymnastics antics, he would talk down to his opponents, often with some Ali shuffles and a classy dance. Ali would "float like a butterfly and sting like a bee." He brought beauty, elegance, and confidence to one of the most dangerous sports on Earth: boxing. He later became a super world heavy weight champion, and I owe him my respect forever.

You can radiate the same level of confidence or even command a higher level of confidence. It is in you to decide which path you want to follow. You can do better at all times. Your confidence can take you places. It is one of the greatest asset God gave you. You have to, as a matter of necessity, have a good attitude with confidence. What is your life looking like today? Do you get depressed with events in your life? Do you wake up in the morning ready to embrace the day with confidence? Do you wake up feeling depressed and hopeless? Sometimes people allow their personal problems to dictate their attitude. They fail to realize that attitude is a choice, and one can decide to keep a positive or a negative one. I think the positive one is better.

Your attitude affects your confidence. Every human being has difficulties, challenges, and obstacles that seem very tough. But the difference between those who overcome their challenges and those who get stuck is their confidence.

If Edson Arantes do Nascimento (Pelé of Brazil) had allowed the world to rob him of his confidence and poise, we may never have known the man who is perhaps the most fantastic soccer player that ever lived.

Socrates, another powerful Brazilian soccer player, played the beautiful game with a free and confident spirit. With his confidence he resisted the military dictatorship that ruled his home country for two decades. He played soccer for years, and through his confidence went back to school to complete his medical degree and also earned a PhD in philosophy. To Socrates soccer was a positive force to create positive change. He passed on at fifty-seven. A few hours after he died, his former club, the Corinthians, won the league title.

With credit to his confidence, David in the Scriptures disorganized and frustrated Goliath, the great but uncircumcised Philistine.

Daniel, with confidence, went to deep sleep in the midst of the fierce-looking lions and came out unscathed following King Nebuchadnezzar's brutality and lack of conscience. With confidence, Daniel refused to eat despite warnings and threats to his life. He was on a hunger strike while in detention in Babylon. Even when his associates, Shadrach, Meshach, and Abednego, were put in the fire furnace that was raised seven times its normal temperature, they came out the same way they went in. They strongly believed that a righteous man may fall but will never give up. They were neither intimated nor overwhelmed by the king's military force. Above all they had absolute and supersized confidence in the God they served and never changed their mind despite the risks involved.

Until you overcome the fear of failure and replace fear with confidence, you will continue to be paralyzed at the prospect of taking any risk.

History has proven that failure can be a trigger and bridge to success. Born in 1769 and educated at a military school, Napoleon had the confidence to succeed. He was forty-second in his class of forty-three, yet he went on to build an army that conquered much of Europe. Napoleon became one of the most powerful military leaders in history and the emperor of France.

Albert Einstein, a German theoretical physicist who became an American citizen in 1940, was a very slow learner in school. He did not reach the required standards in various academic subjects. Yet he is considered the father of modern physics. His work, including highlighting the danger of nuclear weapons over time, was affiliated with the Institute for Advanced Study, Princeton, New Jersey, in America. While at university, I read about his work in physics. It is very inspiring.

In his first inaugural speech, Franklin D. Roosevelt said, "The only thing we have to fear is fear itself." Failure is never the end; you can begin again. No matter what you are going through, be it distress, low energy level, cancer, persecution, depression, poor endurance, loss of a job, low morale, famine, back pain, stroke, or lack of money, the truth is this: You are more than a conqueror. With confidence and by pressing forward with determination, you will always overcome. The key is: Do not be afraid. Be confident. Make changes, re-arrange your plans and believe and move on. Once you believe with God on your side you will see positive changes.

Barack Obama, a son of an African immigrant, believed in his confidence, and today lives in history as the first black president of the greatest and most powerful country in the world: the United States of America.

I read of a young man in America who is a rare example of a confident man. Paralyzed by a cardiovascular accident (CVA), aka stroke, at the age of thirty-two, he can barely write or pick up objects with his hands. Despite his limitations he graduated with an associate degree in paralegal studies, earned a bachelor's degree in law and society, and had plans to attend law school at fifty-two so that he could advocate for the physically challenged.

When I decided to employ my late mother's example of confidence, I stopped doubting my instincts. I flushed out all the bad energies in my relationships. I blocked every negative influence in my life. As I started to have faith and put more action into myself and my dreams while taking risks toward expanding my capacity, I experienced a rapid growth of faith in myself. I am very grateful for faith because it assures me that we have a God who hears us and loves us. Whatever you put out into the universe comes back to you. Be true to yourself, and never let anyone tell you how to think, intimidate you, or regard you as a second-class citizen, ignorant or illiterate. You are a first-class citizen. It is up to you to display your poise. Let people smell, see, and feel your positive energy.

Radiate confidence with joy, and your confident and positive energy will always come back to you in an abundance of peace, love, happiness, and fruitful expansion.

Confidence breeds fearlessness. Rather than carefully testing the water, dive into life with absolute confidence and reckless abandon. Create and imagine and boldly commit to it with all aspects of confidence and drive. Couple this with prayers and a forgiving heart. Forgiving cleans our heart of the deadly poisonous catalog of wrongs done to us. It opens channels for abundant blessings.

Studies have shown that people who commit to a cause and follow it diligently have a higher percentage of success than those who have lots of vision but never commit to their cause. Believe in yourself, embrace love, keep a good heart, and take time to explore wherever you go while keeping focused with confidence. Discover a new passion and go for it. You never know if that will skyrocket you to greatness. Confidence also breeds self-esteem. Love yourself and admire all parts of your body, not just your face. Be grateful for the way you were created.

Studies from the University of Canterbury indicate that a high level of confidence can protect and enhance heart health. Confidence can lower your heart rate, hence putting less pressure on your body and helping you think better, focus better, and then take bold steps to reach the heights that God designed for you.

Positive reinforcement from family and friends can also build one's confidence as well. It can restore self-worth. Confidence allows you to learn from your mistakes, flops, and successes. Learning to pick yourself up after a fall is the instant way to re-fire and inch toward success. When you fall, you never stay stagnant. There must be mistakes before success. You can attend all the success seminars, read all the success manuals and books, and watch every celebrity mentor series on TV but still not be excluded from mistakes. However, the price for success must be paid in mistakes or shortcomings. No one has achieved anything without paying a price for it. Some pay with their money, energy, relationships, or freedom, and some have paid with their lives. There is always a price to pay for success. Are you willing to sacrifice anything?

Star baseball players only get a hit about four out of ten times. This is a high failure rate. But by focusing on their averages, they believe with confidence that by swinging the bat they will get a hit. The same thing applies to life. Life is about swinging, no matter how many times you fail to get a hit. If you fail to make a hit you try something else and aim for another hit. Even when you fail and feel you have lost direction, you can always get back on track. It is in you power to bounce back. Do not ever let lost opportunities or mistakes discourage and keep you away from creating things. With confidence you can bounce back, and it will be very easy for you to step up and take on another project. If you believe and act with faith God will always get you back on track. He has done it since the inception of mankind.

The way God works is similar to using the general positioning system in your car. Despite setting the GPS to your destination location, with distractions, you may miss your turn. Then the GPS immediately recalculates with reference to your present location and eventually gets you to your destination. God acts the same way. He is always giving you directions and will always bring you back on track, even if you miss your exit or get lost. He will always re-position you. Just believe.

Making time for people who matter most in life also enhances success. Keep a few close friends and tap into their wealth of knowledge while helping them as well. Stop rolling from person to person, for a rolling stone gathers no moss. Make better friends and connect to them, for they constitute a positive force toward greater opportunities. Shift your focus from controlling people's stupidity; rather, create your own happiness. Start a new project, embrace new ideas, and build new useful relationships. Watch what the future holds rather than traveling the hopeless dead end road of changing someone whose stupidity you cannot control. Above all run far away from toxic people. Immerse yourself in people who posses positive energy, support you from their heart, and are willing to celebrate your success. Dedicating yourself with your whole heart means believing in yourself, your dreams, your aspirations, and believing you will achieve. Believe that, even when you have hundreds of "nos" to every master plan, you will break through one day.

Even the Chicken Soup for the Soul book was turned down by many publishers. Believe with your whole heart and do not be downcast. Keep pressing on. Do not be scared of what may happen tomorrow.

The same forces that took care of you and the situation yesterday will take care of you today and tomorrow until you exit the world. You will be shielded from harm and be given the fortitude to overcome. So keep away from your mind all anxious thoughts and hopeless imaginations but rather have a positive attitude and faith that you will overcome.

Apostle Paul was at the peak of his career when he was put in prison. He was never discouraged nor disappointed. He picked up courage and wrote almost half of the New Testament in the Bible. Even in the most depressing situation of life, Paul was very creative.

LITTLE CORNER:

"You are the most solid and confident person on Earth, and you are a reflection of the confidence you charge into the atmosphere."

THE POWER OF GRATITUDE

GRATITUDE IS APPRECIATING WHAT YOU HAVE. Gratitude is appreciating what you have now. Gratitude is appreciating anything you had in the past. Gratitude is appreciating in advance something you will have in the future. Gratitude is being contented with what you have. Gratitude is being thankful. Gratitude is being grateful.

Those who understand the power of gratitude will benefit absolutely well from it in their life time. Gratitude is the ability to be thankful for the things we receive on a daily basis no matter how small. The ability to be grateful is very crucial in one's life. Gratitude and love are interwoven and always related. Oftentimes it is very difficult to distinguish one from the other. Gratitude can lead to feelings of love, appreciation, gratefulness, and overwhelming happiness. It breeds generosity and compassion, which rewires the brain to fire and release more positive energy. An interesting study has shown that the brain is not fixed in a certain way but can adapt to stimulatory changes. The human brain can be reprogrammed (also called rewiring or recharging) and involves the ways each neuronal cell is linked to another. Emotions activate these neurons, hence triggering a reinforcing feeling of positive thought. These then enhance powerful and positive habits.

The power of gratitude has always existed. Gratitude has been practiced since the onset of life. It is still growing and will always grow. Our thoughts and feelings affect our lives. Negativity, which means ungratefulness, breeds depression, anger, fear, and even failure. Being ungrateful breeds negativity, depression and can be poisonous. Deciding to be grateful generates positive feelings. Everyone has the power to feel good and be grateful. The happier you are, the more you find things to be grateful for. Be grateful, be happy, start feeling good, be kind, get excited, and be motivated. The more grateful you are, the more energized you will feel, and the more you can achieve. Mathew 7:7 says, "Ask and you will receive." Will it not do your soul some little good to be grateful for receiving and receiving whatever you have asked for? I am very sure it is the right thing to do.

Gratitude is the ability to be grateful. In other words, gratitude is giving back. Gratitude is showing joy. Gratitude is saying "Thank you" even when you don't feel like. It is the power of showing that you really appreciate things. Gratitude is a powerful force. It is the greatest energy in the world. The more grateful you are, the more blessings that come your way. I have learned that each time I say thank you, I receive blessings equal in amount to the depth of my gratitude. Gratitude can be practiced in different ways. It is not just by being grateful.

When that small child at the line in a store waiting to buy candy asks, "How are you, sir?" be grateful for the recognition. If that gas attendant pumps gas into your car, be grateful. When the store manager forgives you a declined debit card transaction for two-dollar bananas two days after payday, be very grateful. If your co-worker buys you a bottle of water on her way back from lunch, be grateful. If someone pulls out of the parking space fast enough so you can park, be grateful. When your friends motivate you to buy that new iPhone to match up with your enlarging networking and business capacity, be grateful that you have encouraging friends who are committed to seeing you grow and succeed.

If you are blessed with humility, be very grateful, for humility is one of the greatest attributes of human character. Be grateful for what you had ten years ago, what you have now, and what will roll into your territory in the future. Be grateful for your parents who nurtured you from birth to adulthood. Even if he or she is not alive today, still be grateful that someone cared about you and is watching over you.

Be grateful for the studio apartment you lived in before that state–of–the-art mansion that you have now. If you are in the United States, be very grateful despite the high cost of mortgage, rent, or the car you are financing. Stop stressing about the rights that you are denied. Do not lose sight of the fact that you are blessed to be living in the greatest and most powerful country in the world. Africans, Europeans, Asians, Oceanians, and South Americans all dream of visiting the United States at least once in their lifetime.

Be grateful for your health every single minute if you can. Nothing can buy or replace your health. Nothing equates to your health. Your health is your greatest gift. It is your greatest asset. It is your life's insurance. Be grateful for health.

Be grateful for your teachers and for the schools, colleges, polytechnics, and universities you attended that made you what you are today. Be grateful for the journals, newspapers, and magazines that you read. Be grateful for people who make you laugh and happy, for they are the awesome and beautiful people who make your heart warm.

Be grateful for all the apprentices and junior staff that obeyed and respected you while under your supervision. They could've been very disobedient, making your job a nightmare.

When you fly, please be grateful for the engineers who built the aircrafts, for the air hostesses that serve you in-flight food, for the pilots whose expertise and precision fly you to your destination. Even though you paid for these services, it is still okay to express your feelings of gratitude.

Be grateful for the street cleaners that keep the streets tidy. Be grateful for the construction companies that repair our highways. Be grateful for the seniors in your neighborhood who offer their wisdom and have dedicated decades of loyal servitude to your community. Be grateful for love. Be grateful for the corner store that makes it easy for you to pick up that box of cereal and milk when you need it most. Be grateful for money for your purchases. Be grateful for that credit line that bought your Mac-Pro computer, which you will pay off later, oftentimes with no interest rate for one year.

Be grateful that during Hurricane Sandy in the Americas in October 2012 you were safe. Be grateful for the first responders who put their safety and life on the line, running into danger to rescue and provide safety. Although they were doing their jobs, still be very grateful for their presence. They made life easier during "Sandification."

There is always something to be very grateful for. Can you see with your two eyes? If yes, thank God. Can you see clearly with your prescription glasses? Be grateful that you can afford the glasses and now have two sets of lenses: natural and scientific lenses. Has your hair fallen out because of chemotherapy? Please be grateful that you are able to receive treatment. Some cannot afford or do not have access to medical care. If you cannot sleep after three o'clock at night thank God you have a bed. You are not alone. Studies have shown that 45 percent of the world's population have trouble sleeping very well at night. So chill; you are not singled out. Instead of complaining all night, be grateful and positive and use that sleepless time to plan the next course of action of what you want in life. The truth is this: people who get what they want are those who try many projects without giving up. They especially plan at night when everything is quiet and calm.

Be grateful for water and food. Be grateful that you can drink, chew, and swallow without a nasal-gastric tube. Be grateful for electronic mails, for text messages, for fax machines, for Twitter, for Facebook and their usefulness to connect. Be grateful for information, for life, for good friends, for the good people you meet on a daily basis.

Be grateful, be grateful, and be grateful. When you are grateful, you are saying that you are thankful and are opening up more opportunities for more good things to flow into your life. You are creating avenues that will enhance your life and can help you succeed.

I know a very young, beautiful woman who grew up under the guidance and strict supervision of her very poor parents. Life was very rough at the beginning; oftentimes Esther had no food on the table. To compound matters further, her father died shortly after she gained admission into a prestigious university. Despite the financial constraints, challenges, and limitations, Esther was endowed with humility and intelligence. The death of her father and the abject poverty she found herself in neither deterred nor changed her gratitude frequency. Esther did a gratitude dance on a daily basis. She wrote on a piece of paper a long list of every single thing she was grateful for and recited them daily like a poem.

She continued being very grateful and oftentimes composed and sang songs expressing her gratitude. She was grateful for little things like seeing the airplanes flying in the air despite never having flown in one before. She filled her life with gratitude. Over time she made good friends at the university. As one friend got to know her better, she was invited and introduced to that friend's rich parents. That was the turning point in her life of immense gratitude. As she told her story to the parents, not only did they understand and connect with her situation, but they placed her on scholarship. Her life changed, she was more grateful, she rejoiced more, slept better, studied better, and today she is a university graduate and happily employed. As a token of her gratitude, she paid it forward by relocating her mother to a brand new two-bedroom apartment. Esther is a living example of gratitude.

The more gratitude you discharge in life, the more happy and blessed you are. The more energy you radiate, the more love you have, the more people will like and want to work with you and can assist in opening doors for you.

When life drops bitter leaf into your mouth, rather than being, angry, depressed, and infested with hopelessness, find something little that you are very grateful for and magnify that feeling a billion times. Then follow it up with a gratitude song and watch the situation snowball from depression to projection.

As a practical exercise, let me illustrate my point. Stop reading this book now, and take a look at the hand with which you are holding this book. Take a look at your cell phone—I know it is by you, but don't text or call anyone yet. Take a look at your comforter that keeps you warm in winter, then your TV, then your academic certificate hanging on the wall, then your child's picture, then the light that you can see with, and then take a look at the roof over your head. Step toward the window and view the beautiful trees dancing, the birds singing in the trees, and the blue sky. Understand that you have all these things, including the blue sky, because you can see and feel them now. Are you not feeling grateful now? Don't you feel better? That is the multiplier effect of a grateful heart. Put your gratitude frequency in action and watch how things will change for good on your behalf.

If you don't have to take a medication to sleep at night, be grateful. If you don't have to force your smiles or take a medication to smile, be grateful. If you do not have to take a medication to be excited, be grateful.

If you have only three pairs of shoes but cannot afford to buy more, be grateful for your three pairs of shoes. Some people have prosthetic legs and are forever grateful for their prosthetic legs and are taking big risks and making big impacts in the world.

The key to enjoying your life and being very productive with a view to succeeding is to find something to be grateful for every day. Write a list of all the things you are grateful for, and read them daily in the morning with a smile, a feeling of affirmation, and a grateful heart. This simple but powerful exercise will give you confidence and keep your attitude positive every day. Never let a negative attitude discourage you from keeping your heart warm with gratitude.

Studies have shown that people who radiate gratitude are more likely to be happier and more likely to live longer. One powerful way of expressing gratitude is by volunteering. Volunteering can elevate happiness levels and increase the release of "happy hormones" in the body. Researchers have shown that helping someone else without thoughts of gratification can relieve pain, stimulate the immune system, and improve well-being. People with a grateful heart feel better physically, emotionally, psychologically, and intellectually. They live longer. They are happy.

Happiness is gratitude, and gratitude is happiness. The bottom line is to be happy and be joyful. If music makes you happy, slot that CD and play it and dance every step, no matter where the beat takes you or when the music ends. What could be better than a song that freshens your soul? That's up to you to love dancing with gratitude and to love what you do. When you laugh, laugh with excitement. Laughter creates a good feeling and peace in your heart, boosts immunity, and reveals our true personality. It lightens your spirit. It is medicine of its own.

To imbibe the power of love as a function of gratitude also means to love your enemies. Loving your enemies means banishing fears, insecurity, jealousy, frustration, and anger. All of these create bad blood and increasing blood pressure. These are your real enemies. It is a very hard task for some people to love their enemies, and they have good reasons for not doing so. It does not matter what wrong people did to you. What matters is the magnitude of the burden of carrying the resentment around. This prevents you from living a productive life full of love, abundance, generosity, peace, and longevity. It takes a toll on you spiritually, emotionally, and mentally. For the sake of life, we must love, forgive, and move on. We learn lessons from being hurt and get wiser. We release from our memories the person who hurt us, wish them well, and replace their spot in our hearts with a positive force.

As this new force emanates, we feel the peace of life within; the brain rewires itself into more positive networks. Once this happens, you focus on what you want to create, be it wealth, love, happiness or even an invention. The whole body feels renewed, energized, and refreshed. Life becomes more meaningful and sweet. I have always believed that the best way to take revenge on people who wrong you is to forgive them, move on, and rebound with great success. Forgiveness brings peace of mind and is always the best revenge.

The greatest people who have ever lived have told us that love is powerful. Thinking gratitude is a way of thinking love, for one cannot radiate love without a grateful heart. It does not matter what you do, where you are, or who you are; the power of love is so important. It is the power through which we connect with people. Love, according to the Bible, conquers all. It changes things, it can create wealth, it reduces stress, and it is a ticket to beauty, to energy, to excitement, and to peace of mind.

Gratitude brings your whole mind into close harmony with the creative energies of the universe. All the good things you already enjoy have came to you along the line of obedience and gratitude. Gratitude leads your mind out along the ways by which those good things come to you. It will keep you in close harmony with powerful creative thoughts and prevent you from falling into competitive thoughts with anyone.

Gratitude brings happiness. The path to happiness is rarely easy. It takes time to develop. With strong and constant gratitude, not just when you like to be grateful, you can attract any force to yourself, including all the good things you have ever imagined.

Oftentimes our gratitude isn't strong and constant, and we are only grateful when we think about it. That is wrong and unfair to the Universe. Ninety-nine percent of the time we are distracted by the engaging events of daily life, and we totally forget to be grateful. When that happens, the supply of what we receive is very limited. We begin to think competitively rather than wait for our time. And when we do that, we shut off the tap and negate the powerful universal flow of events. We then experience the type of universe that we believe it is, and that is what we get. If you believe that there's not enough, then that's what you get. Period. How can gratitude solve this? It's not that hard to understand. If we're in a constant state of strong gratitude, we're focusing on the things that are going right for us. From that we can begin to see that the universe is always there to supply in solid abundance all that we need to excel. This is the law. Having an attitude of gratitude and being joyful have their own benefits. God wants us as mortals to be abundantly happy and carefree. He expects lives to be lived at their fullest blast no matter the circumstances. By doing so you are vibrating in consonance with the evidence of faith, an unseen but positive force that surmounts all challenges.

If you concentrate only on the positive side of every situation, event, or challenge, you will soon discover that your whole life will be radiating only positives. You will be filled with gratitude, a feeling that keeps you happy and fired-up, a power food that nourishes the soul.

Happiness is a sister to gratitude. Happiness is a natural medicine. You might say, "I am not such a happy person; I don't laugh much." It is true that we are created differently, but if you stand in joy, happiness, and gratitude, you can stand very strong irrespective of what's going on in your life. You have the power to train yourself to be happy and laugh over two hundred times a day like a child. I advise you to be happy always, for you never know who is falling in love with your excitement.

But it is very imperative to note here that some people are still trying to find happiness the wrong way. People attempt to find happiness instead of giving happiness. To have happiness, one must give happiness. Happiness is like table salt. It can heal, it can preserve and enrich, but to have all these effects, it must be sprinkled around. If it is kept in the shaker and not sprinkled, it is of no effect. This means that one must sprinkle happiness in order to receive happiness. When you do so, it is inevitable that happiness comes back to you. It is like sprinkling cologne on others. It's impossible not to get a splash of it on you.

Never allow the pressures and stress of daily life to deny you of your right to have gratitude and joy. Stress is part of life. There are good and bad stresses. Good stress is the type of stress you feel when you see you family member doing very well at a competition. It is that stress you feel when you receive an unexpected amount of monetary gift from a friend. These are good stresses and they benefit your body positively. The most important thing is how you react to the stress. Your decision now will be to look beyond problems, limitations, and frustrations of life, and instead be happy, be joyful, and have an attitude of gratitude. When you do so, then ask God to fill your life with his supernatural peace and the spirit of gratitude so you can live large and carry on with the beautiful life the universe offers. Then you can stretch your mind with a new project, experience, or vision. Then you can raise your own bars and raise them higher as you work toward your dreams.

One of the easiest ways to be happy is to give. Giving, no matter how small, is medicine to the soul. Experience has taught me that giving is a form of noble gratitude and that it brings happiness and good things.

A few years ago in winter, a young woman was walking in very cold weather to her new job. I knew her because she had worked at a local supermarket where I shopped. She had always greeted me politely and made nice jokes whenever I shopped. It was not a coincidence that I had taken the same route in my car. I had driven past her, but seeing her from my rearview mirror, I pulled over and waited until she got to me. I asked if she needed a ride, and without hesitation she jumped into the car. You see, not too long before, following my immigration to the United States, I, while struggling, had walked to work on foot. I had appreciated it when someone who knew me was pleasant and offered a ride to save me from the freezing cold. I wanted to extend to her the same courtesy I had rarely received.

I took her to her workplace and gave her a bottle of water from my car and a twenty dollar bill. I thought that if she did not have the money to pay for a taxi or bus to work, then she might not have money to pay her way home. I assumed the money I gave her would come in handy when she punched out from work eight hours later. She was extremely grateful and said it was the nicest thing anyone had done for her all week. I was sad that she had already been walking for about twenty minutes, was very tired, and seemed to be catching a cold. But I was very pleased to have had the opportunity and the rare privilege to be in a position to give. The act humbled me and made me feel fantastic.

Giving does not have to be monetary. Recall what Peter gave to the lame man at the Beautiful Gate (Acts 3:6): "Silver nor gold I do not have but what I have I'll give. I command you to stand up and walk." Peter did not give money here. He gave what he had at the time. He gave hope. He gave purity. He gave healing. Your faith may not be as strong as Peter's to be able to heal, but you can always find something little, no matter how small, to give to someone who desperately needs it. As soon as the lame man received strength in his muscles and bones and was able to walk again, he started praising God. In essence he was very grateful. That is gratitude. You can only imagine how Peter felt in his heart after this noble act. I believe his heart felt very warm and his blood pressure could have lowered by at least five millimeter mercury (5mm/Hg).

When you give, you are not only adding to people's joy but also sowing seeds. You are sowing good seeds to God's people. If you learn to give your best to people who need them the most, God will also sow in your life and give you his best. He will expand your horizons.

Oprah Winfrey, in continuation of her giving exercise, built the one of its kind Oprah Winfrey Leadership Academy for Girls (OWLAG) in South Africa.

Her aim was to give poor but very intelligent students an opportunity for academic excellence. Not only is the school creating future academicians, it is also packaging leaders for South Africa's tomorrow. These girls were the first real South Africans born around the time Nelson Mandela was released from prison. They never experienced Apartheid.

Thando Dlomo, Debra Ngcobo, Mashadi Kekana, and Bongeka Zuma were among those in the first graduating class and are now pursuing various degrees in liberal arts in American colleges. They were full of joy and gratitude. They called the school founder and benefactor "Mama Oprah." At the first graduation ceremony of the school, Nelson Mandela, former South African president said, "We hope the school will become the dream of every South African girl." It was amazing.

But you don't have to build a school in Durban, South Africa, or champion a movement for the homeless in America to be a giver. You can always give something, even on the job, at school, at your church, or in your local community. You can buy your co-worker a cup of coffee on your way back from lunch. You can visit those senior citizens in your community. You can help clean their apartments and run some errands for them. You can also have a full conversation with them. You can open up your heart by listening to them and their life stories and experiences. Guess what? You have no idea how much you will be appreciated, and you can also learn from their wisdom. In this way they can bless you immensely as well.

I encourage you to have every reason to be grateful for being here on Earth. See the world as a very friendly environment and not as being against you. The universe is positioned to support, bless, and enhance you, but you must be willing and ready to radiate a positive attitude. Complaining is very easy, sometimes fun, but it is needless when compared with the benefits of having a grateful heart and creating a plan for positive advancement.

Life is what you put in it. If you desire to be happy and grateful, then happiness is yours. If you are sad all day, then the negative forces overpower you with sadness and hopelessness. You have been endowed with every positive force to swim out of any difficulty. You are like the stream that does not force to push its way into and across the solid mountainous rock but finds a way to navigate around it and flow on. That's you, but you got to have that mindset. There is always a way to be grateful for any bad situation. Be grateful your car broke down on the highway—at least you have and the ability to drive that car to where it broke down. Give thanks at all times, and feel grateful, for it is the right thing to do.

LITTLE CORNER:

"Give thanks at all times, and feel grateful, for it is the right to do."

THE POWER OF INNER PEACE

PEACE IS THE ABILITY TO BE at ease with one's self, body, and soul. The role of a peaceful mind as a tool to success cannot be over-emphasized. Peaceful people are at ease and relaxed. They are more likely to bounce back from life's disappointments and can forgive easily. They have low incidence of high blood pressure, low depression level and anxiety. They are slow to anger. They move on with their peaceful existence more easily. They don't replay videos of their life's mistakes in the YouTube of their memories. They do not nag, complain, or become frustrated. They live life one day at a time. I have always believed that every being on Earth has a quiet, calm, stable center within them that is never disturbed. It is one's responsibility to find this serene center within and escape into it periodically for rest, renewal, inner peace, and reinvigoration.

Oftentimes people feel guilty when they are not doing something. They don't realize that rest is a vital force in life. The same way our body tires out after prolonged physical activity is the same way the brain tires out after doing activities nonstop for a long time. When the brain and body are overworked, they tire out, lose vigor, run short of energy, and may collapse. The more exhausted we are, the more narrow and short-sighted our visions are and the more we are stressed out. This is why stressed-out people are uneasy, hyper, and less productive. To be more productive, the body first needs inner peace to relax, meditate, dream, and visualize. Today I challenge you to find that inner peace in you; find that quiet place and meditate. You may feel wary and uncomfortable at first, but over time the benefit comes. Take some time off to unwind and cool off. Take five deep breaths now; relax in your innermost peaceful area. Do you feel better? Fantastic.

Meditation is another key to rejuvenating the soul. He who never meditates is like a person who does not look in the mirror and, unaware of being untidy, goes out to a function looking unkempt. Meditation directs our thoughts to God, the manufacturer of our lives and tries to correct our faults, moderate our impulses, and fine-tune our conscience. Meditation does not have to last for two or three hours. Ten, twenty, or thirty minutes can be a good way to start. It worries me that people cannot shut off their phones, TV, and every other electronic gadget for just ten minutes to be quite for a while and be at peace and nourish their souls with meditation.

Successful people meditate and rest very well. Rather than working tirelessly from day to day, they replay their successes, achievements, and accomplishments within the inner peace of their being. Rest relaxes the body and makes the body more productive. Some employers offer two to three ten-minute breaks to their employees. This way they are restful and energized to do better. Researchers have found that employees are more productive with breaks and, as such, have enough time and energy to work harder. Also related to rest is sleep.

Certain foods have been found to enhance sleep, thus keeping the body energized to do more work. Nuts, seeds, and some dairy products contain the amino acid tryptophan, which plays an important role in mood and healthy sleep.

Everyone on Earth seeks inner peace, inner love, freedom, health, power, and, ultimately, wealth. How you perceive yourself, your reality, and the environment is the number one step to inner peace. This later translates into inner awareness and then inner power, which translates to outward action and, ultimately, wealth.

I have realized that some people in general do not understand the importance of inner peace. Even when they do, some do not practice it. Studies have shown that people with inner peace are calmer, more focused, better organized, and more successful. The power of inner peace is so intense it can help you achieve anything you want on Earth. It is so powerful that once it is tuned to the right frequency, whatever you conceive and believe is achievable. The principle is very clear.

When you are able to think and imagine with inner peace, the subconscious self has a way of creating it, and making it possible. Our minds can develop and create powerful things for us. If you know how to use it, it can generate powerful vibrations that radiate the right positive energy into the universe. This energy will come back like a boomerang to you, creating exactly what you expected. Inner peace has incredible powers. In order to achieve the things you want in life, you must first take control of your inner peace. People use it to actualize their dreams. They are never afraid, they take the perseverance attitude to the highest level, they act consistently, they exhibit the no-quitting attitude, and they achieve.

We all have power in our inner peaceful existence that we can perceive. All you have to do is tap into the abundance of what you already have and see the effects manifesting in your life.

Inner peace has been found to be interrelated with happiness. Happiness enhances life. I have learned that the only way to have inner peace is to be happy from the inside. People have come up with great dreams that were shattered and allowed their setbacks to ultimately knock them into the den of unhappiness. They settle for the mediocre lifestyle and decide to live to just get by. Although goals are different, I have found that everyone has something in common. That is the desire to be very happy. Unfortunately, many people go through life without being happy. This is a negative energy, and it breeds failure in its entirety. When you are happy, your inner soul is at peace. Once that happens, the body is tuned to a very powerful, resonating frequency that connects the universe to emit strains of good things, success, wealth, blessings, love, peace and more happiness.

Is your life tuned to the happiness channel or Stress Channel? If it is the later,then you have to change channels. If your life and emotions are tied to stress, you can even feel it in your eyes, nose, stomach, your neck, and your whole body. If you continue to be stressed-out without changing the channels, you will continue to have stress and give more importance to the stressful situation, thereby losing sight of the solution. You will be sad, edgy, angry, and less productive. You may be hurting your arteries and blood vessels, hence predisposing yourself to high blood pressure, obesity, cancer, and even stroke.

Stop stress by taking time to unwind and rest. You can also make a habit of eating walnuts, a wonder nut that has been found to reduce stress. Walnuts are loaded with omega-3 fatty acids, which may help the body cope under stressful conditions. In a study conducted by Penn State University, subjects were made to undergo two types of stress tests: one in which they submerged a foot in ice water, and the other in which they had to prepare a short speech in a very short time and then deliver it in front of a camera. The participants showed significantly lower blood pressure during both activities when they took the tests after eating 1.3 ounces of walnuts and a tablespoon of walnut oil daily for six weeks. So you see the power of walnuts in calming stressful situations. On the other hand, if you are depressed, it is advisable to exercise regularly and eat lots of healthy fats like olive oil. Stay away from foods with high trans-fat content, often found in fast foods. Trans fat is bad for the body and has been thought to interfere with neurotransmitters, hence distorting the brain's natural chemical equilibrium. Both stress and depression can impair productivity and slow the pace of success. I teach these things in my Fitness classes and the effects have been wonderful amongst my members.

Studies have shown that happier people do better in trial-and-error situations. They have been found to even do better in problem-solving challenges. Happy people are energetic, they are enthusiastic, they are filled with solid self-esteem, and they are powerful. They are creative, they are loved by people, and people want to be around them. They make decisions and take actions with a happy heart. Even when they fail, they bounce back with a happy attitude. How happy are you?

It is important to point out that the act of being happy is not a day's program. It is a long-term feeling that requires total commitment and positive views to things around you. But one thing is very clear: Achieving success may still not bring happiness. It depends on how you feel and react to the wealth that follows. Riches may not bring happiness to one's life. I strongly believe that prosperity enhances lives only if it is used to attract love, peace, and fulfillment to us and in the service of others.

How can one always be unhappy when they are searching for happiness? Maybe they don't understand the meaning, or they are looking in the wrong places. Oftentimes people want to get the best job, a sexier body, a nice car, nice supervisors, a perfect partner, or buy that forty-two-inch television to watch the Super Bowl before they can be happy. Happiness has a lot to do with what is going on in the inside. It pertains to doing things rather than having things. This is the power of inner peace. It is devoid of envy or competition. Once it flows, it is propelled by wanting to help oneself or even helping others. It breeds a feeling of accomplishment, it soothes the nerves and calms the body, and, as discussed previously, it can even reduce high blood pressure. Researchers have found that when we act within the limits of our moral compass, coupled with inner peace, then there is love, progress, and happiness.

One aspect of inner peace I have found to be a very useful catalyst for success is the power of adequate sleep. Do not underestimate the importance of sleep. Diabetes, high blood pressure, and heart disease have been linked to sleeplessness, mood disorders, and obesity. Good sleep patterns can be practiced by simply going to bed at the same time and waking up at the same time each day. Exercising helps with sleep. Avoiding caffeine and not eating heavily before going to bed also help keep you sleepy at night.

When we are asleep, the mind, body, and soul are at peace and in accord with one another. Sleep rejuvenates body cells, rearranges worn-out tissues, and ultimately keeps one very healthy and in the right frame of mind to think. A body deprived of good sleep over time becomes disorganized and disoriented. Current studies show that the average person gets between seven and eight hours of sleep a night. While sleeping, the body goes through a phase of sleep called REM (rapid eye movement) every sixty to ninety minutes throughout the night. During this time the brain is very active in processing and initiating its repairs. When this sleep cycle is lost and/or interrupted and sleep is lost, it takes a toll over time on the human body. Brain function is impaired, metabolism is affected, including weight gain, and it could lead to a host of medical problems.

When we sleep well, the body repairs well, and there is a subsequent perfect functioning of the body. Although the body has a way of making up for lost sleep by way of micro sleep, adequate sleep on a daily basis enhances proper body functioning and ultimately can lead us to think properly, engage in meaningful activities, and achieve success. Sacrificing sleep can also weaken the immune system, affect productivity and cause weight gain. It can also cause migraine headaches. Studies have shown that lack of adequate sleep increases the likelihood of being overweight and can cause other illnesses like heart disease. With lack of sleep we tend to be hungrier in the morning, which can cause us to eat more, hence loading on useless calories that cause weight gain. Over time the weight of the body can cause undue pressure on the knee and ankle joints and can lead to osteoarthritis of the knee, excruciating pain and can cause impaired gait.

Lack of sleep can also slow the metabolism of the body. This can be avoided by staying away from caffeine and sleeping at a regular time daily. Eat and don't stay hungry, for hunger can cause migraine headaches. Avoid skipping meals, play some sweet music, and read your spiritual books. Keep your mind off of worries. Fill your mind with those things that radiate peace, love, positive energy, nobility, purity, and happiness. Your mind will be at peace, you will sleep better, and you will think better on ways to improve your life and be successful. This is a proven experiment.

Sleeplessness can make people do unimaginable things. I read about a man who was so sleepless at night that he started cleaning the whole house. Not only that, he disturbed his neighbors in his building, and he ended up throwing away many vital things he should have kept. At night useless thoughts can race through your mind like an off-the-track race car. You wake up sleepless in the morning and feel very tired. There is total exhaustion, which impairs daily functioning. It can also cause excessive hunger. Rather than worrying and cleaning the house at three o'clock in the morning, I suggest one can turn the situation into a very productive night by communicating with your creator in absolute quietude. You can plan things as well.

Prayers are also another powerful factor in achieving success. Prayers create peace, especially when they are answered. All over the world, in almost every culture, people pray, in groups or alone, in churches, mosques, temples, holy places, mountains, at home, in school, and even in the kitchen. Prayer connects humans to the spirit being; it's a sacred link to their creator. It opens doors to success when said and practiced the right way. It worked for me and can work for you.

Refreshing your mind can help in creating your life. Researchers have shown that mind exercise slows the aging process and can even delay the onset of certain diseases. Studies have shown that moderate exercise, like brisk walking, benefits the body. A healthy body is a happy body. Exercise strengthens the bones, muscles, tendons, and ligaments. It can ward off diseases. It rejuvenates the body.

The American College of Sports Medicine recommends thirty minutes of moderate intensity exercise at 60 to 74 percent of the maximum heart rate five days a week or twenty minutes of high intensity exercise at 75 to 85 percent of the maximum heart rate three or more days a week.-ACSM 2000

During exercise, the heart is constantly pumping and the sweat glands secrete sweat while flushing out impurities from the body. As a result more oxygen and nutrients are delivered right to the brain. During this process the body secretes protective chemicals that initiate the growth of neuronal cells in the brain. With a healthy body, one tends to think better, process better, and work harder toward achieving life's goals. Exercise may delay a disease long enough that the symptoms may not be seen in a lifetime. With good exercise and a diet of mainly plant-based foods, one can reduce the chances of getting diabetes or being hit by a bout of heart disease, especially those who are genetically connected with the traits. Exercise produces a feel-better mood physically and emotionally. The American Institute for Cancer Research estimates that about 38 percent of breast cancer cases could be prevented by maintaining a healthy weight, eating right, exercising regularly, and drinking less alcohol. With diabetes, losing belly fat is the key. Keeping an ideal weight can enhance the body's ability to use insulin, the hormone that regulates blood glucose into cells for body metabolism, hence lowering risk of type 2 diabetes. Exercise boosts energy, lowers anxiety, and improves blood pressure. Exercise is medicine on its own.

Reducing body weight also lowers blood pressure significantly and may reduce the risk of cardiovascular diseases. Dropping just a fraction of your weight can have a tremendous impact on your overall health. Exercise has also been proven to help with depression. People who best handle stress and depression are those who work out and exercise a lot.

For women, especially postmenopausal ones, strength training is very important to replace muscle mass lost over time. A few days of working out with dumbbell weights or participating in other weight training activities will help to maintain and build strong muscles. For my clients during my Fitness Training classes, I often recommend stretching to improve flexibility and mood. Eight to ten minutes of stretching every morning is the key. However, you can choose the schedule that suits you.

But whatever you do, find time to exercise. Exercise protects the body against diseases like stroke, diabetes, and even colon cancer. Take a walk during your break time on the job. Park one hundred yards away from your destination, and walk the rest on foot while swinging your arms in a rhythmic fashion. Use the stairs and avoid the elevator. Not only are you walking against the force of gravity, you are building very strong leg muscles and bones as well. As a fitness trainer, I advise my clients to wear a pedometer on their waist to measure the number of steps they walk each they. I advise them to strive to hit at least eight to ten thousand steps a day. I add variety with a little cardiovascular challenge, like running or bicycling, to maintain good health and ward off illnesses. A sick person is sad, has no inner peace or joy, may not think well, and could make poor judgments. In addition they could be impaired in making important decisions, which could hamper progress.

LITTLE CORNER

"The American Institute for Cancer Research estimates that about 38 percent of breast cancer cases could be prevented by maintaining a healthy weight, eating right, exercising regularly, and drinking less alcohol."

THE POWER OF NEGATIVITY

NEGATIVITY IS SIMPLY THE ATTITUDE OF not having a positive attitude. Negativity can be a catalyst for failure. Negativity also includes speaking, believing, and acting negative Negativity can be caused by many factors. One of the most common causes of negativity is limited belief. A lot of people are infested with negativism, either due to their limited belief in themselves or just unbelief in their potential to achieve. Another cause is simply negative belief. For example, often-times people become preoccupied with a life of frustration, anger, and resentment so much that they lose sight of the importance and benefits of simply being positive. They see their life as messed up, unhappy, and worthless. They believe the universe has singled them out for failure, and with time their lives becomes filled with negativity.

Negativism can also be caused by associating with people, family, or friends who are negative. When we do they can affect how we feel. Eighty percent of the time we are with other people. If they are negative, being around them can influence you to be negative. They can make you unhappy by exhibiting negative thoughts and behaviors. They may not believe in your dreams and may poison your attitude. It is very easy to be infested with negative thoughts, especially when most people or all the people around you are negative in their orientation, thinking, believe and actions.

Events of life can also cause or lead to negativity. People handle things differently—some with a positive attitude and others with a negative attitude. The latter complain, feel angry and hopeless, and get stuck in their circumstances.

The workplace is another area that can be infested with negativity. It can be counterproductive by affecting the energy of the workers and therefore becoming very detrimental to the organization as a whole. Negativity in the workplace can be seen in the workers' general attitude, in the way they do their business, how they relate to and speak with co-workers, or the way they react to changes in their organization. With the world economy undergoing several changes, most organizations are making drastic modifications in their organizations. These may be positive or negative. It could be downsizing, lay-offs, or reassignments. In most cases the negative attitude arises when these changes do not favor the staff. Someone who is very sad, unhappy, and dissatisfied about his job may not put in his best toward fostering the image and progress of his company. Even in a near perfect situation devoid of lay-offs, negativity can still be present as a result of lack of self-esteem or lack of confidence. The negative worker may feel intimated by other co-workers and may feel second-class. In this situation everything coming from the organization may seem not right.

The effect of being negative can be very detrimental to life, health, and general well-being. Negativity can affect blood pressure in a bad way. Negativity in an individual can create unhappiness. It can cause one to lose faith in the universe. It can create emotional imbalance.

Negativity can cause anger as well. When one is always negative, there is a tendency to be angry, and nothing seems to make the person happy. When that happens, frustration occurs even in simple matters of life. It can attract more negatives. It can create an unpleasant lifestyle. It slows down your progress. It can also affect judgment.

It's common knowledge that like attracts like. So when your life is full of negativity, there is a chance that you will be attracting more negatives. If you continue to complain and find negatives, over time the mind tunes itself to the negative frequency such that your whole life, present and future, is full of negatives.

The easiest way to get rid of negativity is to turn any negative feeling into a positive feeling. It is very easy to have negative thoughts, especially in a world full of wars, joblessness, poverty, and crime. To counter the negative attitude, the best thing to do is to find good things that have happened in your life and dwell on them for days. This will help alleviate the negative thoughts. Understand that constantly thinking of bad situations led to your negative attitude. It is also okay to be happy, level-headed, and calm, even in very difficult situations. The more often you are frustrated and angry, the more you are working up your system, which can cause your blood pressure to go up. If your negativity is caused by people around you, it is okay to move away from them or limit the number of times you communicate with them.

The first thing I did when I realized that my life was being influenced by negative people was to flush many of them out of my life and limit my communications with the others. The moment I did that, my life took a new turn. I started seeing lots of positive changes, and I felt relieved to be separated from the negative bondage. I even heard the opportunity to immigrate to and live and work in the United States. I changed my attitude to reflect positivity. I picked up positive projects that engaged my time. I made a positive move and moved on. Things changed big time.

Understanding the harmful effects of negativity is another way to stop it. Knowing that every cause has an effect will help reduce your negative thoughts. Knowing that the effects of negative thoughts can be detrimental will help you avoid negativity.

Finally, try to replace any negative thought with a positive one. You will be on the road to creating a positive lifestyle and the type of good life you want for yourself. You will create success.

THE POWER OF POSITIVITY

IN SCHOOL WE LEARN ABOUT INFORMATION and how to give it back to our teachers as answers to pass examinations. But in life, real education consists of taking learned knowledge, thinking about it positively and seriously and oftentimes critically, and then producing something brand new with it. Everyone has potential. You are a smart thinker, but you may not have realized it. The brain is an explicit center for thinking and creating. Solving big problems comes from thinking positively, but you have to have a healthy brain too and the willingness to use it to think as well.

The same way we try to keep fit by eating healthy is the same way we nourish our brain with brain food and exercise. Certain foods are beneficial to the brain as well as the body, and a healthy brain thinks better. Blueberries, blackberries, and strawberries have been found to be beneficial to the brain and also help prevent age-related memory loss. They also have powerful antioxidants that help change the way neuronal communication occurs to improve cognition. A healthy brain thinks well and positively. Studies have shown that women who eat more berries regularly have brains that function a little better than non-berry eaters.

The way, how, where, and what we think is directly related to the extent of our success. Thinking brings great ideas. Oftentimes the ideas are sharp, unusual, and can be a good step to initiate success. Ideas can create a powerful campaign for progress. It can promote articles for advancement of an astonishing project. It can even make a powerful change in your local community. You do not have to be an activist for social change or build a massive project on Wall Street to make a change, but you can always start small. You can always make a change.

I am a very strong believer that the first step to excellence can be initiated right in your own kitchen. Whether you live in New York, Addis Ababa, Bangkok, Dhaka, Lusaka, Paris, Osaka, or in a tiny village in the KwaZulu-Natal province of South Africa, there is always a golden opportunity to think and bring to life great ideas. Your ideas can make a positive impact not only in your life and in your community but also in your country and on humanity in general. You may even be so powerful that your friends and community might end up watching you being interviewed by Oprah Winfrey on TV. Just think how cool, solid, and rewarding that could be.

Our thoughts and mindset affects things in our subconscious. They could be positive or negative thoughts. It all depends on what you are thinking. Positivity creates positive results. Being positive before setting out for that job interview is a sign that you are convinced that you have the position. When you are positive, the forces of attraction in the universe will open various ways for you to land that dream job. Even when there are other qualified candidates, the magnitude of the energy in the person with the most positive thoughts about the job will attract the job to himself. Belief in having a parking space in advance will offer you a space in the parking lot. Each time I think seriously of money, I end up receiving a check in the mail or an offer from someone to buy me something or a nice gift. When you emit the frequency and vibrations of positive thoughts, the law of the great universe will move things, love, people, and even abundance in human wealth in your direction.

Positive thinking is a very serious mental attitude that transmits into the mind's thoughts, words, and pictures, which ultimately transmit into growth progress, advancements, and expansions. It is such a very powerful mental exercise to expect good and fantastic things.

Research has shown that a very positive mind radiates joy, peace, success, good health, and successful lifestyles in every situation, action, motion, or path that a person takes. Life is all about setting goals, dreaming, and living positively with a view to having a breakthrough and achieving what you desire. Positivity creates you lives desires.

The biggest breakthrough so far in my life on this earth came when I learned how to use and apply my positive energy. The total reformation and reorganization motivated me immensely to overcome all anxiety, be myself at all times, and be more aware of my surrounding energies. Then I flushed out all the negative people in my territory. I was in control of my frequencies, and then I redirected my energy only to positive people and positive thoughts. I was a totally different person. Unimaginable and powerful things started flowing into my daily life.

Life is all about taking alternate paths and switching frequencies. But often we find out that the path we have chosen may not be in line with our dream career path either because we don't have the means to achieve them or because the dreams seem very elusive and unrealistic. The result is that we often give up and resign ourselves to fate. That is why it is very important to take the time to find out what you really want to do to avoid wasting too much time in the wrong arena. One African proverb states, "You don't stand in one place to watch the masquerade entertain," meaning that you have to move around often to catch different views of the whole display. In essence you have to constantly switch life's channels.

To figure out that dream which can change your life, pay very close attention to your instincts, monitor how you feel, and, if possible, write them down on a daily basis. What do you do that makes you feel happy, satisfied, accomplished, and terrific? Is there something you can do without any strings attached to it and you love and enjoy doing even when the situation is very uncomfortable? If you make a move and feel connected to it, you had better stick to it and pursue it. These simple and oftentimes ignored principles are the cues and signals that could propel you into that passion mode to strike to realize your dreams. Just follow the path with all your energy, your love, and your time, and go wherever the road leads. Even when the road hits a detour, never give up. Find a way to navigate through the corner streets and into the major road with a view to continuing your journey. But be very aware that the road to finding and pursuing your dream may not be that simple or easy. No, there may be times when the road gets rough, but you have to be willing to toughen up and brace for the challenges. There is no road to excellence that is completely smooth. If you hang on a little more, you will definitely smile later. Oftentimes victory follows tough time.

The mind is so structured that whatever it sets focus on, expects, and thinks about, it accepts and receives. It is so heartbreaking that only a very few of people living on Earth really believe in the power of positive thoughts. While some think of the idea as garbage, the disciples of the positive dynamism believe it works, and they practice it on a daily basis. Surprisingly a few others who know it still do not know how to practice and benefit from it. Those who practice it have seriously benefited immensely, as evidenced in many books, lectures, authorities, courses, and even in sermons. People who are down and dejected are often advised to think positively, but they seem to brush it aside, believing it does not work. I feel very sorry for them.

Thinking positively brings positive results. I will illustrate this with a true story of two people I know very well. Duncan is a very good friend who is very negative and laid back. Having graduated college, he applied for a job as a marketing executive with a publishing company. Even before going for the interview, he had already made up his mind that he was not going to be successful in the exercise. He believed the job was not for him and that he was not qualified. To cut the story short, he went to bed late the night before the interview and woke up late. He was so shabbily prepared that he was thrown off balance with the highly technical questions asked at the interview. He messed up, he did not get the job, and he lost hope. His negative mindset made it impossible to connect with the power of attracting the job to himself. He was dejected, confused, frustrated, and battered, thanks to his disbelief in the power of positive thoughts.

Esther, my other friend, is a very brilliant, happy, and positively minded young woman. She paid her dues in her undergraduate program in industrial chemistry and graduated with flying colors from a university in West Africa. Because she believed strongly in herself, she went for an interview very well prepared with a laser positive mindset and landed a job. Today she is very well established, and I am very excited about her success. This is the power of positive thoughts in action. It really works for those who believe in it.

The bottom line is this: when the mindset is positive, we radiate pleasant feelings and constructive pictures that shine like golden lights, which brighten the day, induce happiness, and promote success. Health is affected positively, lives are enhanced, authority is maintained, confidence is at the topmost firing frequency, love manifests, and life is sweet. Whether you're an aspiring soccer player dreaming of playing in the World Cup, a young basketball player dreaming of representing your country in the Olympics, an emerging restaurant owner, or an aspiring social critic, there is always a time when you need an extra push and some kind of solid strategy to fire yourself up to an enviable height. But whatever path you tread, seek advice from people. Some people will say, "Nice, powerful, and solid idea," and some will say, "No, forget it. It isn't going to work." You must listen to both parties, feel their energy levels, and understand where they're coming from. Then make your decisions. For example if you want to start a business, take time to consult people who are already in business or do a research on how to start a business, then gather all your information and take the ones you need to kick off your venture.

One day as I was contemplating how to rearrange and foster many of the ideas running inside my head, I ran into a senior citizen taking a walk in the park. I had come to run one lap on the track—my usual weekend routine. Following our conversation as "transient exercise buddies," he read and asked why my T-shirt bore the inscription, "Bringing Fitness Through Charity." When I told him that I founded a program that brings fitness to people through charity at no cost, he said, "Really, you are doing something terrific. You are making a big change." I knew it was the moment to expand my vision. I never knew I was making a big change. A few weeks later, I fired up my determination to launch my own website for my charity at www.calo-burnfitness.com. You can check it out and thank you.

With the website I created a forum for the whole world to see what we do. I started making speeches in churches to give publicity to my charity. I took e-mail addresses of those who cared to join and benefit and sent out weekly newsletters after every workout. My charity started expanding, attracting children, young adults, and even seniors. People gave donations of water for hydration during our workouts. The mayor gave his support and encouragement. People offered indoor facilities for my use in winter months without charging a dime. My charity took a new turn, today has served hundreds people, and is still growing and making an impact. I learned from this experience that seeing the path to the end motivates me to get there someday. But there must be a positive movement. There must be a determination to do what you determine to do with the end results deeply rooted in your mind.

My personal experiences have shown me that visualizing only positive situations coupled with keeping positive perspectives create great success. Smiling often always has its own advantages and enhances positive thinking. I have always advised people through my public speaking to replace any negative thoughts with positive ones at all times. I encourage them to direct their physical and mental energy to good stuff and avoid negativity, redundancy, and self-criticism. I mandate that they focus on positives instead. I make them understand that this is a long-term process and is not learned overnight. It is a gradual process. It is persistent action. It will ultimately train your mind and rearrange it to think only positive thoughts and ignore negative ones. No matter how ugly your circumstances are today, bear in mind that the problem is your perception of the circumstance, and you can always change things around. But one thing is clear: you must act. Action moves people to react toward you. When people see you are taking positive actions chances are that they will want to associate with you and be part of you when you succeed. No matter how infinitesimal the action is, you must keep a positive attitude. Word repetitions have also been proven to be helpful. Word repetitions means repeating regularly with affirmation the pattern you want your life to assume. For me I have always repeated works like- I am Solid, Powerful, Organized, Successful, Blessed, Focused , Ignited to excel. I wasn't surprised when my life started changing for good, receiving blessings and support from everyone including those who do not know me personally. Practicing word repetition will make lots of changes in your life It is like attracting those things to yourself. The changes will come. It will take some time, but change will definitely come and attract the things that you desire. Successful people also have troubles and fears, but they are so focused, on course, and persistent on a worthy goal that they feel it is impossible to turn back, give up, and quit, even when they felt like it.

Positive thoughts are so powerful that it enhances accomplishments. Our actions and feelings are guided by our thoughts, meaning that we control whatever we think. A critical analysis of all the people that you know will signal to you that the positively thinking ones achieve more in life than their negative counterparts. Attitudes, whether good or bad, are a manifestation of thoughts that have been cultivated over years and now deeply rooted in your subconscious mind. It is left for you to decide which one to fire up.

If you are always filled with a negative attitude, It is better you now flush the poison from your mentality and mobility. Switch that channel to something positive, and make a decision to be very productive to enhance your life. Peter and David of the Scriptures made decisions. Oprah Winfrey made a decision. Michael Jackson of blessed memory made a decision.. Recording artists Usher and 50 Cent made decisions. But you don't have to make the same decisions as these superstars. You can start with a decision as simple as exercising three times a week to build not only your muscle strength but enhance your cardiovascular system. What productive decision have you made today, this week, this month, and this year?

Positivity can create toughness in your soul and can trigger success. As such, positivity can shut off all distractions that could be an impediment to reaching your goals. It can create a massive turn around and re-construction of your life. Striking out fear can also lead to success. This is called being tough. Toughness can be seen in the lives of Nelson Mandela of South Africa and Martin Luther King of blessed memory. They believed in themselves, and they had faith they were fighting a just cause. They were determined, they believed, they fought, they achieved, and their names have been carved in gold in the annals of history. I strongly believe that if you analyze it critically all they believed in was their determination that they can succeed. They practiced what they believed strongly in. Success is a result of regular practice, persistence, and constructive initiatives. It is never a matter of how long. It is a matter of hard work, commitment, and dedication.

Positive thoughts attract positive people. Surrounding yourself with positive and focused people makes life easier. Delegating authority is very important. Oftentimes we surround ourselves with positive people but want to be the leader in everything. We want to do it all. In our desire to do the will of God, we may take on too many responsibilities. In as much as it is done with a clear intention for positive results, we end up overwhelming ourselves. The key is this: be positively minded, be a positive leader, exhibit all the positive energy, but delegate responsibilities. Moses spent every day listening to complaints from his loved people until he was told to slow down lest he wear himself out. He was advised to appoint capable people to help carry the load. In essence he was advised to appoint leaders from the positively minded people that surrounded him. That way they could all lead together to achieve more results and never be overwhelmed. In order words we should learn to delegate, release burdens that we were not meant to carry, and instead focus more on what is correct for ourselves. That way the road to success becomes a little easier. Do not be too eager to criticize your thoughts. Avoid negativity and self-criticisms. That is the first step to thinking positively. Change your thoughts to positives today and you are on the road to creating what you want.

LITTLE CORNER:

"Success is a result of the regular practice of persistency and constructive initiatives. There is no miracle involved. It is never a matter of how long. It is a matter of hard work, commitment, and dedication."

THE POWER TO CREATE AND INVENT

EVERYONE ON EARTH HAS THE POWER and ability to create anything, including wealth. Life is about creativity. Every scientific discovery is proof that the human brain is wired for creation and loaded with unlimited power for creativity. The computers we use today came out of one individual's creative thoughts. Everyone has the potential to strive for creativity. We are all endowed with the power to create something novel. Even if you think you can't create, find someone who is creating and support them. By so doing you are creating by induction. Once in the hallway of the business of creativity, your own channel and path become very clear. The joy of life lies in the power of creativity. It is a natural opportunity for every living being on Earth.

Life has taught me that inside every human being lies the absolute power to create anything. Oftentimes we are embedded in procrastination and find it very difficult to set off on that golden path to create a life that can be treasured. People have a hard time using their power of creativity because they see limitations and feel that they are just ordinary. When they do they limit their potentials to be successful.. Everyone on Earth including children, youths, women, men, and even seniors are "pregnant". Yes, pregnant. But I don't mean pregnant with a baby. I mean pregnant with ideas, pregnant with thoughts, pregnant with dreams, pregnant with positive energy and creative ideas, and pregnant with passion. Pregnant with concepts and vision waiting to be born, fed, nurtured, organized, energized, electrified, fired up, and put to good use to change the world.

Oftentimes your vision will be clear. When it is hidden on the inside, it will shine and glow with time as you progress. Have a clear vision of your dreams, and do not allow your eyes to adjust to the level of myopic deficiency rather stretch your creativity and see things move towards you.

What if we could switch things around and give just 40 percent of our time to what we have been created to do? We could be very productive and create things that will not only enhance life, family, and local community, but we could also change the world. It is all about making very good use of your time. Value your time well. Time ticks every second. Time is precious. Every second that ticks drags to minutes, hours, days, weeks, months, years, decades, and centuries. Use your time to develop your life. It takes time to be creative. There are millions of opportunities to learn how to enhance our lives. Reserve your energy for your best use. Use your energy to develop good ideas that God deposits into your brain on daily basis. It does not matter how small they are. Every idea is a gift, every opportunity is a gift, and every day you live is a gift. Everything you have is a gift. Even your voice is a gift—use it to sing. If you can't sing like Usher, Akon, Jennifer Hudson, or 50 Cent, at least sing to yourself or sing to the glory of God and he will bless you amazingly.

Every person you meet is a blessing. It is up to you to make good use of these daily opportunities without limitations or a "shut down" mentality.

In 1900 the head of the US Patent Office was ready to shut down the office. He thought that almost everything humanly possible had been "created" and invented. If his plan had gone through, today we may not have cell phones, iPads, digital recorders, laptop computers, iPhones, hybrid cars, Mac-Pro computers, microwaves, or electric fruit juicers for your smoothies, to name a few. That would have limited us so much in the beautiful and great America and the world we live in today. The same thing applies to the human mind. We apply the same "shut down of our human patent" and close the mind factory and stop inventing new ideas in our lives. I call this "bankruptcy of the human mind."

Born in February 1847, Thomas Alva Edison was a powerful and successful American inventor and business mogul. Thomas, in his lifetime, created and developed many devices that powerfully influenced and enhanced the life of people around the world from generation to generation. His work included the motion picture camera, photography, and the everlasting, practical electric bulb (which he developed and lit where I wrote this book and live today, Roselle, New Jersey). Over the years since his death at the age of eighty-four in 1931, numerous projects have been established to honor and immortalize him. The Thomas Edison State College was built in Edison, New Jersey, and today makes it easy for adults to pursue higher education while expanding their capacity and exploring the school's degree programs. Also the Thomas A. Edison Career and Technical Academy offers classes in construction technology, health science, automotive engineering, hospital services, and retail instructions for high school age students. Do you see the power to create things here?

In October 2012 Serge Haroche of France and David Wineland of the United States, both sixty-eight years old, received the 2012 Nobel Prize for inventing methods to observe the bizarre properties of the quantum world. A quantum particle is a particle that is isolated from everything else. Their research led to the building of extremely precise clocks and has also helped scientists to take the first steps toward building very fast computers. What a power to invent.

In my little empowerment speeches, I ask people if they would like to be rich, and they will stare at me as if I am joking. "Yes, I want to be rich" is the reply I often receive. If you want to be rich, you have to be committed to be rich. You have to stretch your mind to discover the possibilities of things you could do to bring success that could amaze you. You have to start thinking rich, believing you are rich, shinning rich, talking rich, and acting rich, and then find your passion and work on it with all your energy, time, enthusiasm and dedication. By doing so, the great power of the universe, the "Law of Attraction," will ultimately open doors to bring wealth. It could be political wealth, emotional wealth, academic wealth, or even financial wealth. You could also create financial wellness and even physical wellness. The power is all in your mindset. Human minds are the most powerful magnets for attracting anything. The frequency you tune your mind to determines the type of life you live. It is analogous to tuning the TV channel. If you tune to channel 24 there is no way you will be watching channel 48. That is how it works in life. With a positive mindset, you can create positive things. Conversely, with a negative mindset you can create a life full of depression and disaster, and you set yourself up for failure. Positive thoughts create positive signals in the brain. This generates positive results.

If your mental picture and outlook is so negative, then you can change the channel by thinking positive thoughts. The correct frequency of thought once emitted into the atmosphere will create anything you channel it to, be it love, peace, job promotion, academic appointment, gift of a new watch, a shoe, a car, a belt, a new dress, or even massive wealth. It can even attract families to remember you and place that unexpected phone call to brighten your day. You can call it telepathy if you want. I call it "Creative and Attractive Force."

Another force in creation is the power of focus. For the body to function optimally there must be a connection between the mental and emotional self. When this connection is lacking, the physical structure, your body, suffers. The innate phenomenal power of focus is so amazing that it can create anything if practiced the right way. If you focus on good things, you create more good things. In this way, while attracting pleasant things to your life, you emit more good energy to the whole world and create more things for people to benefit from. Once that is kicked into motion, the universe will be affirmative to support and align your life to more goodness, success, more happiness, progress, and anything positive you desire.

Nothing in this world comes from the outside. Everything originates from within and the feelings from the inside. Your thoughts, mind set and inner feelings are the creative force of all things. I call it the "Creative Positive Force" The creator of the universe has endowed us with an abundance of abilities to enhance our lives. The trick is in thinking big, feeling big, hoping big, believing big, and, devoid of any thought of lack. Creativity is synonymous with hard work. To be creative, you may have to work extra hours, even if it entails giving up your weekends and leisure, family, and friends for a while. Having a "whatever it takes" mindset will enhance your ability to explore and create your life's blueprint. It entails commitment, and with providence you can rebrand your life. Once you are on that path, the universe will assist you, protect you, guide you, enhance your skills, attract the right people, and can even initiate unprecedented miracles. But commitment is the key factor here. You have to be ready to commit and make sacrifices.

Creative thoughts can initiate creative actions. We can create the type of life we want to live. We can make it happen. Being in peace with ourselves can enhance our success. Creating happiness is one important factor in creating success. One important part of life is finding and doing what makes us happy. When you do what you love and have a passion for it, your life will be filled with excitement, you wake up daily feeling excited to go to work, not crawling throughout the day with low energy. When you do what you love, it creates an avenue for love and peace of mind and opens ways for you to excel. Being at peace with what you do is like a magnet. The more you are at peace with what you create, the more you attract good things to yourself, and the more you grow.

One important thing to mention here is that in order to create, one must be healthy, for without sound health, human function can be limited. Good health is a very powerful asset. It is the most wonderful insurance you can have. Physical fitness, walking, running, good food, reading, meditation, and prayer are all imperative and restorative activities that recharge the human body. What are you doing to recharge your body? What are you doing to nourish your soul, replenish your energy, and enhance your being?

It is very simple to recognize people whose lifestyle is of optimal quality. They incorporate total fitness as a condition to improve their life, enhance cardiovascular endurance, boost their energy level, and maximize confidence. They are socially sound, mentally balanced, psychologically arranged, spiritually empowered, and physically fit. They work hard without any fear of crashing because their health is sound and firing at the highest frequency. Even when they are sick, they recover and bounce back quickly. Their solid health improves their performance goals. Their target is ultimately to achieve. It is imperative to note that a sound body is a hard working body. Physical fitness influences quality of life, improves health, and creates a positive energy toward achieving one's goals and aspirations.

As a Fitness Trainer I have learned that diseases are another serious factor that inhibits people from being physically active and from reaching their target goals. These can be prevented with regular checkups, health awareness seminars, physical activities, and regular and healthy eating habits. On eating habits I always advise my clients to stay away from are starchy foods. I advise them to eat food with good calories and also load their stomach with colorful veggies and fruits and other types of fiber. Having at least seven hours of sleep daily, relaxing with absolute quietude, and staying off drugs, cigarettes, and limited alcohol consumption, to mention but a few are good ways to enhance health as well. Studies have shown that regular physical activity can lower the risk of certain diseases, including hypertension or high blood pressure, osteoarthritis and rheumatoid arthritis, diabetes, and even some forms of cancer. It can reduce obesity, osteoporosis, and can improve overall fitness. In the Bible, 1Timothy 4:8 even states that "physical training has some value."

With an improved and healthy lifestyle, one functions properly, thinks well, adjusts better to life's stressors, and ultimately makes better decisions and can plan better.

I am a strong believer in the premise that we can create the type of life we want. The truth is that people who get what they desire are those who search for what they want. It is your responsibility to strive to better yourself while improving your attitude on a daily basis. This is possible once you devote to making small personal moves regularly. I will illustrate this more clearly. The first step in recreating your life is to clearly cut off all the things you don't want. There is a fine line between what you want and what you don't want. When something is wrong with your creative thoughts, simply discard that which is wrong. I have noticed that most human beings have "Complaint Syndrome." They earned their bachelors degree in complaining, their masters degree in complaining, and their doctorate and specializations in complaining. Their life if full of complaints. Even when things are going well, they complain. That's the first thing you want to get rid of. There is always a time of resistance and discomfort in people's lives. Even babies have a way to stop discomfort. They simply cry and roll over, signifying that something is wrong. They spit out that food either because they are full or it doesn't taste as good as the previous meal's food. If a baby can do this, why can't adults? To avoid complaining when you feel discomfort, just smile, laugh, take a deep breath, and then think of the next positive move to counter and recover from your "Complaining Syndrome." Complaining eats from your time to think and create things. It kills your creative skills.

Another powerful factor to excelling in life and creating things is the desire and knowledge to explore possibilities. I have always motivated people to take a step forward, release fault-finding energy and imagine and explore opportunities abundantly located in their daily lives. I advise they imagine things. There is power in imagination. If you feel sick working in that hospital as a direct care nurse, imagine being the director of nursing services, or, better still, imagine finding a job in another hospital for a change of scene. If you think you have been in that miniature office for donkey's years, and it is getting on your nerves, then visualize working in a bank, at a big restaurant where you meet and network with people, or even working with Donald Trump or becoming a TV show producer or even speaking publicly. These may seem impossible at first glance, but you will be amazed that the only way to discover the limits of the possible is by pushing past the impossible and exploring beyond the safe borders. Once you do that, things become clearer. Oftentimes it requires pushing away from your comfort zone to achieve big things.

Prioritizing plans after exploring possibilities is another important aspect of creativity. If you stay mute while looking at the possibilities, you will notice that you will lose them to other people who are willing to take the opportunity. Think, believe and explore the priorities, and then slowly bring them into tune with your mind, heart, and soul. Then ask the universe to bless them. Then take action. Taking action does not mean the plan will work. If it does fine, then congratulations. If it does not, try plan B. Plan B might be that force that skyrockets you to stardom. The key here is to never give up in trying and believing.

I read of a former systems engineer who teamed up with his wife, a former science teacher turned garbage collector. They run a business making goat's milk soap from their home, with all their twelve children helping out part-time. Today they have produced over two hundred thousand bars of soap, and they make lip balms, lotions, and even laundry soap. Imagine the power of goat's milk and the thought process of shifting grounds and imagination. You too can do the same. I say you can even do better. Yes, you can.

There is a creative power in everyone. Even when we make mistakes, we can also recreate and bounce back. Oftentimes when people make mistakes, they get down on themselves and think, "If only I had done this differently." At this point people may feel downcast, depressed, hopeless, and useless. Don't let anything stop you from creating a new energy to progress. No matter how many times you have blown it, or how much you have messed up, you can always bounce back. Just believe.

History informs us that most of the greatest people on Earth, and even in the Scriptures, made many blunders in their lives but came back. Paul started as a murderer. But his end story was mightier that his mistakes. He became one of the greatest leaders that ever lived. Above all he enacted the "power to excel" and by recreating himself and writing half of the New Testament he became a powerful apostle.

The key is this: Our mistakes, failures, and dangerous choices should never keep us from recreating things. It does not matter how, where, or when you started in life. It is about the way you end it all. Never let your dream die. You may fail, but you keep learning from your failures. When you learn, you grow. That's what it is. It does not matter how many times you fail or how many times you keep getting up. Once you stay down, you're done—it's a wrap. Once you have put your acts together and ready to move on then ask the universe to assist you in recreating your life. You will be amazed by the result.

Oftentimes the universe places people in our lives to assist in this creative process. Ruth, in the Scriptures, was downcast after the death of Mahlon her husband. She was bereaved, battered, barren, and broke. I call this the four *b*'s. But she recreated her life. How did this re-creation process happen? She chose Naomi as a close and reliable confidant and said, "Wherever that you go, I will go, wherever you lodge I will lodge, thy people shall be my people and thy God my God. (Ruth 1:16). In essence she was saying, "I will hang around you. Be my mentor." It did not matter that Ruth a Moabite was a Gentile and Naomi a Jew, nor did the difference in their age or social status matter. Doubtless there were times they disagreed and never worked together. But when God wants to align you with someone, he will plant somebody with a totally different ideology and experience in your life. Naomi was the light by which Ruth saw again. She tutored, advised, mentored, and counseled Ruth. She poured out her heart and assisted her in reaching her new and wonderful destiny. She recreated her life, got out of her comfort zone, stepped out into a massive aura of faith. Ruth started enjoying life again, living large with a positive attitude, and ended up marrying Boaz, who owned a large expanse of land. She later gave birth to Obed who became the father of Jesse who was the father of David. Do you see how Ruth bounced back and went on to become a member of the family of King David?. What a turnaround.

Excelling in life oftentimes involves connecting with the right people that the universe sends to help solve your challenges. Most times it is advisable to have a mentor. A mentor guides you and offers you insider opinions on navigating your process or dreams. They give an opportunity to tap into your skills with a view to providing the solid foundation for growth and a successful life.

Shortly before my dear mother went to be with the Lord in 2004, she said to me, "Son, I want you to develop an attitude of gratitude, and please give back and give at the slightest opportunity." I took that advice and ran. When I started my fitness and wellness charity in 2011, I knew I was creating something new and in line with my mother's philosophy. The idea was not born out of a desire for money but from the burning vibe to help others who are willing to connect with the opportunity. The charity started with five people on a sunny Saturday morning at the park. I knew the program would be a powerful movement, but I never knew it would grow so quickly. On a daily basis I garnered the help of one or two people who are willing to connect with the movement. They put in a little time and energy. I sacrificed focus, time, money, and commitment to support my charity. Initially I was a lone ranger, and I met lots of stumbling blocks, but with a vision and a mission to give back, I fired on with fortitude. Today Calo-Burn Fitness, my charity, has served hundreds of people who benefit or have benefited from my free fitness classes. When people ask why the program is a charity one I tell them, "I asked God to fill my heart with charity—the greatest gift of all times. He did and gave me a gift. I don't want to mess up that gift. I am enjoying it. It has changed my life, blessed me, honored me, and it has given me incredible energy." We are still expanding, changing, and impacting lives through this charity initiative. To create change, one must be willing to be changed. It's human nature to get tired of repetitive actions.

But with perseverance, changing course, and steadfastness and believe in your actions you will overcome.

LITTLE CORNER:

"I asked God to fill my heart with charity—the greatest gift of all times. He did and gave me a gift. I don't want to mess up that gift. I am enjoying it. It has changed my life, blessed me, honored me, and it has given me incredible energy."

USING YOUR POWER TO EXCEL

THERE IS AN INNATE POWER AND drive for survival in every human being. Even animals are endowed with powers to survive. In Africa's wild forests, when a zebra wakes up in the morning, it is aware that it must run faster than the tiger or it will be consumed. Conversely, when the tiger wakes in the morning, it is aware that it must run faster than and catch up with the zebra, or he will have no food for the whole day. But in humans it does not matter whether you are a tiger or a zebra. The key is to look through the window, know exactly when the sun rises in the morning, and then start running to achieve and create things for that day. That is the only way to be productive and to excel in anything.

On a daily basis opportunities and good ideas are presented to us and signal us to start something powerful. Sometimes we are so reluctant to start because there are obstacles that hinder the kick-off. We delay so much that the ideas and opportunities die with us. But here is the key: the best way to make any big dream a reality is to start in some little ways to give life to the ideas on a daily basis. These small ways prepare you to embrace the big dream when it knocks on the door. It is always very easy to step into big dreams when you are already getting a feel of the dream and have prepared in little bits. When that golden opportunity opens up, you will be more than ready to embrace it and run. In other words, live your dreams little by little on a daily basis. It does not matter how much time it takes to come to fruition as long you are constantly living it. Live your dreams.

Oftentimes human powers are so hidden that it takes absolute desire and drive to tap into them and use them for success. The power in us enables us to discover, to invent, to manufacture, and to create. It enables us to succeed.

Great scientists have made great inventions through the power in them. They not only believed in their power, but they acted on it, and the results followed.

There are almost seven billion people on Earth today, and only a handful have been able to apply the use of their innate power in their life.

In this chapter I will share a few daily tricks to apply to your life in order to enhance it toward achieving the lifestyle that could improve your life.

But first, I will give a few general recommendations. As a personal trainer I advise my clients to engage in regular physical activities, reduce salt intake to lower blood pressure, and reduce their two *w*'s: weight and waistline. I tell them to avoid sugars, such as corn syrup, high fructose syrup, maltose, and malt syrup, and to read food labels before buying at the supermarkets. Palm oil and butter are bad fats that have serious consequences on health by increasing the level of bad cholesterol (low density lipoproteins, or LDL; "L" is for "lousy"). Eat the good fats, such as olive oil, flax-seed oil, and those found in avocados and seeds. Eat fish and nuts for their omega-3 and omega-6 contents, which is good for the heart. Eat lots of berries for their powerful antioxidants and health-boosting properties. Buy and use a pedometer with an aim toward walking ten thousand steps a day.

Over time I encourage my clients to do strength training and resistance exercises at least once a week for thirty minutes, comprised of two sessions of fifteen minutes with a break in between. This develops strong bones and healthy muscles, which enhance metabolism and help burn more calories. I engage them with a cardiovascular workout that raises their heart rate a little. Cardiovascular exercise is any exercise that gets the blood pumping, heart beating, and the sweat glands sweating, like running, dancing, jumping, etc. It's important to drink lots of water to remain hydrated. I remind them that exercise boosts energy, enhances self-esteem, and provides empowerment to plan better and do better. Finally I tell them that weight loss reduces blood pressure and may lower the risk for colon cancer. It is very important to understand that without the right energy level, one may be limited in the things they can do. Exercise improves energy levels.

The power to excel in life starts every morning. Your success is a function of your daily planning process. I have always advocated waking up with a smile on your face, stretching your whole body, meditating for the day, and performing about ten sets of breathing exercises to circulate oxygen and increase blood perfusion. The moment I wake up, I smile and affirm that it is going to be a brand new day full of energy, peace, success, and blessings. After breakfast I pop a piece of gum into my mouth to stimulate my facial muscles and also to improve blood supply to my brain as the vessels contract and dilate. This makes me smile better, keeps me in a good mood, brings peace, and enhances my day.

Next I take a glass of water on an empty stomach and then give thanks while getting ready for the day's activities. This keeps my mind at a very positive frequency and energized to face the challenges of the day. I second it with a balanced diet consistent with all the three basic food nutrients: carbohydrate, good fat, and protein. I like a little sprinkle of cinnamon powder and a spoonful of olive oil on a slice of whole wheat bread. Studies have shown that cinnamon improves mood. If you are the coffee-drinking type, then half a cup of mildly caffeinated coffee can stimulate you for the day. They all increase good mood feelings.

I have never neglected the importance of inhaling fresh air first thing in the morning. Fresh air improves mood by refreshing the body and supplying oxygen to all the body tissues, hence enhancing respiration. Oxygen enters the human lungs during inhalation of air and then passes through the part of the respiratory system called the alveoli and into the lungs. Then it is bound to the oxygen-carrying substance in the blood called hemoglobin. This oxygen-loaded blood is then delivered by the action of the pumping effect of the heart to the muscles. This blood oxygen diffuses into the muscle cells and takes a trip to the cell mitochondria where it is used in the production of the primary source of energy needed for human function called ATP (adenosine triphosphate). This is the energy that carries you into your daily functions, energizes you as you go through your daily chores at work, home, church, in the field, or even at the track. More and more oxygen breathed in regularly goes through the same process to supply all your needed energy for a very productive day. A body depleted of energy cannot think properly, organize daily tasks, or be productive. In other words regular oxygen intake is a very powerful activity that enhances life and creates strength in order to work hard toward your success in life.

Listening to good music daily can also enhance your life. So can the sounds of nature, such as the birds singing in the early hours of the morning and the trees moving and shaking to the early morning breeze. These little things put you in a happy mood and will energize you to kick of the day with a smile. Over time it becomes part of you and influences your life to be more productive and energized on a daily basis.

Feeling good is another powerful way to enhance success. Even when things go wrong, keeping a positive attitude will improve the situation.

It will enable you to realize your mistakes or even learn from your mistakes. You must be changed in some way. Either the situation makes you tougher, or it makes you sober, more humble, and more sympathetic to others in similar situations. With a positive attitude, your problems will never leave you disappointed but will enhance and empower you to fire on full cylinders.

Giving is another powerful force in creating success. Studies show that giving improves mood. Giving open doors of opportunity. This includes giving back to your community. You can hold food drives for your local food pantry or volunteer to clean the apartment of a senior citizen. You can organize toy drives for that struggling new kindergarten school in your neighborhood. Or, on a larger scale, promote or sponsor a boot camp to enhance physical fitness of people in your community.

Oftentimes lots of people are caught up with the time they are putting in for others. By focusing some of your effort on helping your community and giving back on a small or large scale, you are not only expanding your capacity, but you are also creating an opportunity for great returns. You will become popular as well. What better way is there to stand out in your community while expanding your capacity? You never know who is watching. We are taught that when you give, you receive. The Scriptures puts it in a more spiritual way: "It is more blessed to give than to receive." I am not talking about giving out all you have. I am talking about giving with your heart no matter what you give or how small it is. This is called kindness.

Kindness touches the human heart and talks to it. A small act of kindness goes a long way, and it does not have to cost much. Kindness sometimes is more powerful than words. It is a divine quality. It is not only interwoven into human nature but is highly appreciated by God, who asks us to be kind to one another. Put in another way, by showing kindness to people, especially strangers, you may be entertaining an angel. This means that your act of kindness might bring you so much overwhelming blessings. Do some random act of kindness today.

Related to giving is service. One of the greatest laws of success is service. Service means giving. We receive what we give. I consider giving as one of the greatest privileges God gave us.. You can give through service, through love, through our work, time, your positive energy or your finances. The best way to give is giving in gratitude from your personal blessings and abundance. When you create a mindset of giving from your blessings, you are creating abundance and a continuous flow of more blessings and prosperity into your life. When you create a mental image of giving, it becomes part of your thought process to give, give, and give. It becomes a practical exercise that creates a life of no limitations.

Giving brings abundance of joy especially when you give with love. When you give , you receive.

A few years ago in the summer, I was at a Walmart store to pick up a few equipment. After shopping, as I walked to my car in the parking lot, a young girl in the front seat of her father's car flagged me down in desperation. I stopped and walked to them. In the back seat were another female child, about eight years old, and a grown man in his twenties. Their father spoke through tears telling me how their house has just been burnt down by fire, rendering them homeless. He asked if I could help pay the gas attendant to put some gas in his van. We drove to a nearby gas station, and I blessed them with some gas. Then the eight-year-old daughter asked if I could buy food for them because they had not eaten since the previous night, had no money, and were very hungry. It was 4:40 p.m. We walked over to a nearby restaurant, and everyone, including myself, ate. I paid and gave them some money for their next meal. The little girl smiled and gave me a hug around my waist, the highest she could reach. This little act of giving humbled me, I felt good, and I was also highly honored to be in a position to give. I listened to them, gave them hope, gave them food, pumped life into their van, and moved on. Their "thank you's" never mattered to me, but their happiness did.

Smiling at someone who is depressed is a gift. You are radiating light into his day. A simple noble act of charity to impact others and make a little difference in their lives can be powerful. A text message of hope to a friend with stage three cancer is a beautiful gift. Encouraging young ones to find their passion, to follow it, and to excel is a gift. When you give a tip of one dollar to that gas attendant who pumped energy and life into your car, you are giving. If you buy lunch for your co-worker who is broke and waiting for the next paycheck, you are giving. I encourage you not to be miserly with your blessings but spread them out a little to those who are less fortunate. You are not only blessing them, but you are blessing the universe and yourself as well. You will be creating powerful forces for your own success.

It is a very rare privilege and honor to be in a position to give. By giving you add value to people's lives. I call this "Equity Giving" because you are building equity in their lives. You are injecting life into their system. I am quite sure your reward is waiting for you, because anything you radiate into the universe will settle back into your life. When we give to people, we provide hope, life, meaning, and value. They feel good, and you feel good and powerful.

There is a fine line between giving and spirituality. Giving should not make you broke, as some people believe. Giving expands your life and adds meaning to your existence. You will be rewarded for it, though it may not be by the person you give to but by the supreme powers. You can give money, motivation, time, love or a gift. You can always give something.

I read of an American woman who went on a volunteering trip to Uganda, a country in East Africa. While there, she learned of Ugandan women who had been raped and widowed. Some of their children had been kidnapped and mandated to join militia forces as child soldiers. When the woman returned home, she organized a group of women who joined forces to create music and songs that helped raise money for the Ugandan women. The team was joined by others who felt touched by their story. Over time they raised hundreds of thousands of dollars for the Ugandan women to help alleviate their compounded problems. Don't you think this team of humble women who raised funds for their counterparts thousands of miles away will be fulfilled by their actions? Of course they will be fulfilled and happier. Spirituality is divine and profitable. I have seen it work in others and in my life as well.

Staying connected with the right people that could influence your life irrespective of culture, race, or economic status will also enhance one's success. By stepping out of your comfort zone, there are chances that you might meet new people. People are brought into our lives on a daily basis for a reason. I have learned to tap into the positive potential of people I meet daily. I try to impact their life while learning from them. The more you do this, the more you grow, and the more connections you make. You are not wasting your time; you are making connections for growth, you are expanding your capacity. Strive today to connect with positive people. At the same time, try to be a people builder by encouraging and supporting them to succeed. Success breeds success, and by supporting others to succeed, you are setting the stage for your goals and aspirations to succeed.

Learning different skills from a multitude of people has been proven to be a catalyst to success, be it dancing, cooking, playing or coaching soccer, or even adventurous mountaineering. Mountain climbers have stood on the tallest peaks of creation in the universe. Yet getting to that peak is never an easy task. Such a journey requires training, determination, skills, endurance, and, above all, persistency and consistency. Believing in oneself also creates the power to succeed. Always believe in yourself, do your best in everything and every moment you find yourself in. Even when people ask for your help, do your best to assist. You can even display a dance move before helping. As you do you will be depositing something in their heart. You are creating an image of yourself in their hearts that will not be forgotten. People will never forget how you made them feel on the inside. There could be criticism and blame about how we do things, but that is not your business as long as you put in your best effort and you are doing the right thing. The most important thing is about having the knowledge, knowing the rules involved in what you are doing , applying the rules to the best of your abilities and making a change.

Even if you are learning how to dance on stage despite never having danced before, you are expanding your knowledge. With the right mindset and some practice, there is always so much you can do. I stepped up one day in my local church to sing in front of over five hundred worshipers. I took it as a leisure exercise. It did not matter if I had the best voice or if I sang awfully. I was neither competing in any singing festival nor trying to impress anyone, including my pastor. I was only praising God and building my confidence for future actions. What matters is that I sang in church, and I received a thundering applause and hugs afterward. When we learn new things, the brain changes to match the new knowledge and, as such, cognitive function is improved. This is called brain plasticity. Learning is the best exercise for the brain. Carve out time to learn something new weekly, then daily as time allows. Whether it is stepping up to sing in church, learn to play piano or learning how to play tennis, it is never too late to acquire knowledge. There is no cap on how much you can learn. There are no limitations to your learning potential.

All of God's creation are endowed with special features to succeed and rise higher. Let me take a classic example—the mountain goats. They can climb altitudes as high as ten thousand feet. The winds may blow, a hurricane may strike, and temperatures may drop to below zero, yet the mountain goat keeps rising to the mountaintop. One wrong step could be catastrophic, yet they are endowed with special feet to navigate the mountain. In essence, the message here is that we as humans are already endowed with powerful innate assets like the mountain goats. All it all takes to reach your desired heights is a little pushing forward coupled with a never-give-up attitude. There are times when it seems that the whole world is collapsing on you. Failures are part of life and part of every success story. Life is about experimenting and making honest mistakes. You never know which experiment will earn you a handshake with the president or lead to a Nobel Peace Prize or the title "goodwill ambassador of the United Nations." You never know.

I learn so much from children. I study how they experiment. They fail many times building their toy houses but never quit. But as soon as we grow older, we stop experimenting and accept failures as destiny. We stop taking risks. No, it takes lots of mistakes and failures to succeed in a project. There is no perfect person or perfect situation. Even the people who invented airplanes and rockets made mistakes in the beginning but continued to improve upon their failures. Today we can even travel in jets that fly faster than the speed of sound.

But oftentimes it seems like everything you plan and execute fails. Oftentimes it is your own negative attitude that is killing all your efforts. Instead of losing hope and remaining beaten down, take charge of your actions, fire the next shot, and reenergize the power within you to create new ideas. Then follow up with a good attitude, determination, and an effective positive force, and watch the universe move on your behalf. Life may have its ups and downs, but the universe is never against you. Every single day in the universe is filled with possibilities and opportunities waiting for you to take action to experience its full gift. Keeping your mind refreshed will help you get ahead and grab these opportunities when they come. Keep your mind fresh by reading inspirational and self-help books. Discover the purpose of your life. Successful people have a purpose and focus. Do not deviate from your focus of what you want to do to change your life and impact others. Get out of your comfort zone, attend meetings, volunteer in your community, give back, go to social functions, seminars, churches, and organizations to network with important, focused, and successful people to enlarge your social capacity and connect with people who can influence your life. The victory of success is within reach once you set goals and work toward them. The most difficult task will become easy as you delve into it with the belief that you can solve it no matter the odds and challenges you may face. Make it a goal to find the joy in everything you do. The most difficult task will become easy when you attach a personal meaning to it or make it a passion. I do this all the time and have benefited so much from this simple attitude. Organize yourself and stand out, create a structure for your time and days, set a new goal, and develop a plan to work towards your goal. Re-brand yourself and you will attract powerful people around you to assist you in creating the good life God made for you.

Take new classes and lessons to broaden your horizons; you never know when the classes will fall into place and enhance your success. I know a woman, a beautiful mother of three beautiful girls, with a full-time job who just started taking classes in acting and movie making. She is not wasting her time, rather she is enlarging her capacity, and I will be the first person to buy her first movie. I call this personal enhancement.

Do something positive every day to enlarge your dream. Never mind what people will say or do; it is not their business but yours. It is not about them. It neither about their thinking nor their view. It is about you. Break away from that resistance hindering your power of creativity, run away from your mediocre comfort zone, and take action and you will be on track to rise, shine, excel, and complete that first successful project. The Power To Excel is inside You.

LITTLE CORNER:

"Do something positive every day to enlarge your dream".

45 POWER QUOTES TO LIVE BY.

1. There is no standard formula for success. You are at freedom to create yours.
2. If you try, chances are there that you will succeed.
3. We will not be afraid even if the earth is shaken and the mountains fall into the ocean depths.

   (Psalms 46:2)
4. The action part disables most people. Don't be a part. Take action.
5. Giving warms-up the heart. Give something today and feel the warmth.
6. There is no limit to human achievement. Set your bar higher today.
7. You can be anything you want if you believe in your power to excel.
8. Everyone has power. They are there in you. Discover and use yours.
9. Opportunities are everywhere. Search and you'll find and use them.
10. If you give love you get love but if you give negativity you get negatives.
11. Never lose hope in anything. Rather have faith and believe it.
12. Celebrate every success no matter how little with gratitude.
13. Accept changes with joy. You will make better decisions.
14. There are opportunities to expand your horizon on daily basis. Use them.
15. Every good idea has potentials. Developing it can be life changing.

16. "In my distress I cried unto the Lord, and he heard me"
   (Psalm 120:1)

17. One good thing is to dream, another is to inject action to actualize it.

18. When you make one move you are one step close to achieving.

19. If you wait for the perfect idea before acting. You may not act at all.

20. Successful people think, focus, act, believe and achieve. Model them.

21. Do something today to change something tomorrow.

22. You are powerful, energetic and destined to succeed. Just believe.

23. You can always re-brand and re-write your history. You have the power.

24. There is power both in positive and negative affirmations.

25. Negativity is contagious. It slows progress.Keep away from negative people.

26. Life is like a marathon race. You lead & fall back, another leads & falls back.

27. Hard work is the evidence that you want to be successful. Don't give up.

28. Giving creates joy in the givers heart.

29. Never lose any opportunity to give. Others need your help.

30. Walking improves energy. Walking helps with good sleep at night.

31. The Lord is a stronghold for the oppressed, a stronghold in times of trouble.
   (Psalm 9:9)

32. Every success story is a product of hard work, belief, faith and God's touch.

33. Determination is a sign that if you work harder you'll succeed.

34. I can do it mentality is the best attitude to achieve anything.

35. If you plan, work, believe and pray chances are that you will succeed.

36. The wider your vision the wider the chances to excel.

37. If you're not quick in processing you may not see great opportunities.

38. Limit sugar intake, sugar gives useless calories and causes weight gain.

39. The heavens are telling the glory of God; and the firmament proclaims his handiwork.

(Psalm 19:1)

40. Faith is our belief that God listens and hears as we pray & gives as we ask.

41. Challenges are only but temporary. They never last forever. Just be patient.

42. Succesful people were once failures.They succeeded because they hang on.

43. Love is like an air-freshener. If you spray it you will definitely smell some.

44. The more you help and bless people. The more God helps and blesses you.

45. Some take pride in chariots, and others in horses, but our pride is in the name of the Lord our God.

(Psalm 20:7)

Azuka Zuke Obi the author of The Power To Excel humbly invites readers to email him at caloburnfit@gmail.com. You can also follow him on Twitter @caloburnfit.

He is on Facebook at facebook.com/calo-burn fitness.

For more information on his next book, and to become a member of his Charity Fitness Movement please visit http://www.calo-burnfitness. com, and thank you so much for your time.

www.AzukaZuke.com
(A Movement for Positive Change)

Please remember to post your honest reviews
at Amazon.com & BN.com

You are appreciated for promoting this book
(We are in this movement together)

Audiobook Available @ Amazon. Audible. iTunes.

27804318R00076

Made in the USA
Charleston, SC
22 March 2014